U0925084

我的中国故事

My Story of China

文化和旅游部国际交流与合作局
中外文化交流中心 编

中国社会科学出版社

图书在版编目（CIP）数据

我的中国故事 / 文化和旅游部国际交流与合作局，中外文化交流中心编；夏侠编译．—北京：中国社会科学出版社，2021.5

ISBN 978-7-5203-8481-0

Ⅰ.①我… Ⅱ.①文… ②中… ③夏… Ⅲ.①汉学—文集 Ⅳ.① K207.8-53

中国版本图书馆 CIP 数据核字（2021）第 089872 号

出 版 人 赵剑英
责任编辑 孙砚文
责任校对 沈丁晨
责任印制 王 超

出 版 中国社会科学出版社
社 址 北京鼓楼西大街甲 158 号
邮 编 100720
网 址 http: //www.csspw.cn
发 行 部 010-84083685
门 市 部 010-84029450
经 销 新华书店及其他书店

印刷装订 北京明恒达印务有限公司
版 次 2021 年 5 月第 1 版
印 次 2021 年 5 月第 1 次印刷

开 本 710×1000 1/16
印 张 17. 75
字 数 241 千字
定 价 198.00 元

前　言

PREFACE

“青年汉学家研修计划”由文化和旅游部于2014年创办，旨在搭建支持海外青年汉学家开展中国研究的全球性平台，为各国“中国学”领域的青年人才创造与中国本土优秀学术、文化、教育机构、团体、企业和学者开展交流、合作的机会，为其学术研究提供便利和实质性帮助，通过他们推动各国学术机构与相应的中国研究机构和智库建立长期稳定的联系，实现双方交流互鉴，共同推进“中国学”研究的发展。

《我的中国故事》选取了来华参加青年汉学家研修计划的225位汉学家中45位撰写的文章并结集出版。这些青年汉学家来华研修的课题涵盖文学、哲学、宗教、历史、艺术、语言、政治、当代社会、国际关系等诸多领域。研修形式分为集中授课、专业研修和实地考察。邀请了葛剑雄、张道根、王玉主等著名专家学者为各位青年汉学家开设专题讲座，并与中国社会科学院、重庆文化艺术职业学院、暨南大学、北京语言大学、上海社会科学院、陕西师范大学、浙江工商大学等单位的专家学者一道开展为期两周的课题研究。学习之余，还组织学员到具有历史价值、文化研究价值及民俗价值的考察机构实地参观，切实感受中国的文化和人文魅力。

在书中，45位作者详细介绍了自己与中国、中国文化的渊源，叙述了自己如何走上学习中文、研究中国的道路，从不同侧面讲述了一个个丰富鲜活、多姿多彩的生动事例。书中既有具体感人的故事，也有对跨文化交流的思考和总结，各位作者为传播中国文化，促进中国与世界各国之间的相互了解，做出了突出贡献。

目　录

CATALOGUE

Catalogue

做中阿交流的使者

［阿富汗］艾哈迈德·比拉·卡里尔
阿富汗战略与地区研究中心研究员

我在巴基斯坦生活了 23 年。那时我既不了解中国，也不知道中国是我们的邻居。随着时间的推移，当我上学学习地理的时候，我还记得，当老师说中国是第六个与阿富汗边界接壤的国家时，全班同学都震惊了，都

不相信。我们看着对方，惊讶地说："什么？"于是，我们敬爱的老师在地图上给我们指出了中国，消除了我们的困惑。就我个人而言，这是了解中国的开始。

慢慢地，我的书读得越多，新闻听得越多，对中国的了解就越多。在巴基斯坦的这段时间里，我注意到中国与西方世界、巴基斯坦和苏联不同，中国不干涉别国内政，也不要求别国接受他们的生活方式、准则和价值观。

毕业后，我随家人返回阿富汗并在一家智库找到了工作。幸运的是，我被指派写一本关于中阿关系的探索性研究的专著。这是我在巴基斯坦上大学时就想做的，因为我在白沙瓦和伊斯兰堡的图书馆都没有发现任何关于中阿关系的书。阿富汗和西方其他国家出版的文献大多是阿富汗与其他国家的关系，特别是与苏联、印度、巴基斯坦等国的关系，却没有任何关于中国与阿富汗关系的文献。我查阅了大量的历史书籍，探寻中阿关系的历史，以期填补学术空白。

在收集资料的过程中，我收集到的信息越多，我就越感兴趣，同时，我也沮丧地发现，尽管两国之间的历史联系如此紧密，两国之间的距离却越来越远。例如，阿富汗的两个强大帝国贵霜和赫普塔利（音译）的居民，实际上是从中国来到阿富汗的；佛教通过阿富汗传播到中国；古丝绸之路上全钦（Quan Chian）曾派大使访问巴尔赫，通过这条丝绸之路，产生了更多文化、经济、宗教联系。

因为我研究中阿关系，同时也是一名作家，所以会受到国际媒体采访，还在国际会议上发表演讲并有机会在智库交流项目中访问中国。中国是我访问的第一个国家。随着我对正在崛起的中国了解越来越多，我发现，一个国家实现繁荣靠的是现代化而不是西化。

To be a Messenger of the Exchanges between China and Afghan

Ahmad Bilal Khalil / Afghan

Center for Strategic and Regional Studies, Researcher

I passed 23 out of my 27 years in Pakistan. I neither knew China and nor do had a knowledge that China is our neighbor. As the time passed and when I was in Crade 4, "Geography" was included in our curriculum. I still remember when our teacher said that China is one of the sixth country with whom Afghans have a border, the whole class was shocked and didn't believe. We looked to each other and in utter surprise said "what?" However, our beloved teacher showed us "China" on a map and removed our confusion. Personally for me, it was the beginning to learn and know about China.

Slowly, the more I read and listened about China, the more I gained knowledge and learn Sino-Pakistani relations. Throughout this period in Pakistan, the fascinating thing to note was that unlike western world, Pakistan and Soviet Union, China doesn't want to intervene in the internal matters of others, and doesn't want to persuade others to adopt their way of life, norms and values, the style of their government and never strive to get control of the foreign policies of independent states.

After graduation, my family repatriated back to Afghanistan, and I got a job in a think tank. Fortunately, I was assigned to write an exploratory research book about Sino-Afghan ties. It is what I wanted since my university days in Pakistan.

Because, since those days, I didn't found any book written concerning Sino-Afghan ties in the libraries and bookshelves of Peshawar, and Islamabad. Mostly the published literature by the Afghan, western and others were greatly related to Afghanistan's relations with others especially soviets, Indo-Pakistan and others. Unfortunately, there weren't any literature about China and its relations with Afghanistan. I picked up a bulk of historical books and searched for the historical Sino-Afghan ties to fill the literature gap.

During the data collection process, the more I collected information from here and there, the more the subject became interesting for me, and in the meantime, I was also dejected that how comes the two nations are apart from each other when the historical bonds between them is much stronger? Take for instance, the two superior empires of Afghans namely the Kushans and Hepthalites have actually come from China to Afghanistan; the Buddhism spread to China through Afghanistan; the root cause of the old Silk Road was Quan Chian's ambassadorship visit to Balkh, and through this Silk Road, there was greater incidents of cultural, economic and religious bonds.

Due to my research on China-Afghanistan, I am a published author and interviewed by international media. Spoke to international conferences, and was given an opportunity to visit China in a think tank exchange programme. China was my first foreign destination. I learned a lot about the rising China and it further influenced me that one can achieve prosperity and move on a path of development through modernization but not westernization.

东“泊”梦照进现实

［尼泊尔］马拉

加德满都大学孔子学院讲师

1995 年，年仅 10 岁的我跟随父母从喜马拉雅山的另一边来到了中国。北京天安门的庄严、万里长城的壮观、乐山大佛的奇美、上海夜景的绚烂，都铭刻在我幼小的心里。1997 年和 2001 年，我又有机会游览了昆明、杭州、西安、乌鲁木齐、喀什、深圳、重庆和上海。

还记得第一次参观天安门广场时，把 Tian’an men Square 说成“Tiny miny Square”。爬上了长城，也并不知道少年的我已然成为“好汉”。在乐山心情激动地看到了在尼泊尔自小熟知的佛陀，但当时并没认识到尼中两国在佛教文化联系中的渊源。兵马俑、西安城墙、法门寺等历史古迹以及杭州、西安、喀什这些丝绸之路的重要驿站所蕴含的历史文化含义，对彼时年幼的我而言难有深刻感悟。在拉萨时因严重高原反应受到特殊照顾的我，虽感激中国医生悉心的治疗和关爱，但直到若干年后才体会到其中体现的中国人民对友邻尼泊尔人的情谊。

2005 年，我获得中国政府奖学金，在北京语言大学（简称：北语）学习一年汉语。之后，我于 2006 年至 2010 年在中国人民大学进行本科学习，毕业后又到复旦大学攻读了硕士学位。

初到中国学习，留学生同学来自世界各地，我置身校园仿佛身处“联合国”。我小时候虽曾跟随父母到过中国很多地方，但对汉语仍然非常陌生，于是在留学之初语言成了一大“障碍”。想起我初学汉语的困难，一次尴尬的经历在记忆中挥之不去。有一天我自己到北京城里逛，准备回校的时候很累，于是决定打车。当时在北语已经学习了快一个学期，感觉自己能用汉语交流了。上车后就对司机说：“我要去北京语言大学。”觉得自己说得很清楚，司机却没听明白，来来回回重复了五遍，直到我用手比画出学校名字的汉字，司机师傅才恍然大悟：“噢！北京语言大学啊！”路上我心里一直嘀咕，我们说的不是一样的吗？后来才想起老师在课堂上强调过，说汉语的时候一定要注意声调，声调错了意思可能大相径庭。从那之后每当说话的时候，我都会特别注意语音语调。

在老师和同学的帮助下，一年的语言学习顺利又愉快。开始本科学习后情况又不一样了，班上的留学生非常少，大多数都是中国同学，老师用中文授课，讲的国际关系专业理论知识对我而言生涩难懂，有时课堂上老师幽默的言语引得中国同学哄堂大笑，我们几个留学生却面面相觑不明所以。幸而老师亲和又有耐心，无论我们遇到什么难题都给我们反复讲解，中国同学也在学习和生活上给了我们很多鼓励和帮助。也就是从那时起，我们与中国朋友们建立了深厚的友谊，在越来越多的交往中，我也学习了越来越多关于中国社会和文化的知识。随着中文学习的深入以及对中国社会了解的加深，我开始参与校内外的各种活动，收获了更多友谊，也获得了一些荣誉。

算起来，到目前为止，我人生四分之一的时间都是在中国的北京和上海度过的。在中国留学的八年时间里，中国文化、政治、经济以及各个方面都对我的人生产生了深远的影响。我不仅愈加深刻地感受到中国语言文化的深厚魅力，也亲眼见证了这些年中国经济社会的快速发展。

硕士毕业回到尼泊尔后，我一直从事着与中国相关的工作。我成为一名汉语教师，教过大学本科生，教过中小学生，现在在尼泊尔加德满都大学孔子学院担任汉语讲师。基于教学积累，近两年，我也开始与中国的尼泊尔语专家一起进行关于中尼两国语言文学的教学、翻译、研究工作，进行了很多翻译实践，出版了若干本译著，也助力了多项文化交流活动。古有中国高僧玄奘不畏艰险，远赴西天求取真经，途经尼泊尔，开启中尼两国文化交流之先河。今天，一个曾连天安门广场都不会说的孩子能够代表祖国尼泊尔，在此与来自世界各地的优秀学者们共同探讨如何成为对两国文化交流与合作更有贡献的青年汉学家，这就是我的东“泊”梦从理想成为现实的过程。中国与尼泊尔世代友好，两国文化交往历史悠久，有着广阔的合作研究前景。中国愿与“一带一路”上的我们共享发展经验，共创全面和谐发展，我愿意倾尽自己的努力为两国文化交流事业添砖加瓦。

A Nepal's Dream Comes True

Aneesh Malla / Nepal
Confucius Institute of Kathmandu University, Lecturer

In 1995, when I was only 10 years old, I followed my parents from another side of the Himalayas to China. The solemnity of Tian'anmen Square in Beijing, the magnificence of the Great Wall, the beauty of LeShan, Buddhism, and the night scenery of Shanghai are all engraved in my childhood. In 1997 and 2001, I had the opportunity to visit Kunming in Yunnan, Hangzhou in Zhejiang, Xi'an in Shaanxi, Urumqi and Kashgar in Xinjiang, as well as Shenzhen, Chongqing and Shanghai.

I still remembered that when I visited Tian'anmen Square for the first time, I called Tian'anmen Square as "tinyming square". Climbing the Great Wall, I did not know that I had become a "hero". I was excited to see the Buddha, well known in Nepal, but I didn't realize the origin of the Buddhism between Nepal and China at that time. The historical significance of Xi'an terra cotta warriors, city walls, Famen Temple and other historical sites, as well as the important courier stations of Hangzhou, Xi'an and Kashgar along the Silk Road, can not have a profound understanding of myself at that time. When I was in Lhasa, I received special care because of my serious altitude sickness. Although I was grateful to the Chinese doctors for their treatment and care, I did not realize the friendship of the Chinese people towards their friendly neighbor — Nepal until years later.

In 2005, I was awarded the Chinese government scholarship. After learning

Chinese for two years in Beijing Language and Culture University, I begun the undergraduate study in Chinese People's University from 2006 to 2010. After graduation, I went to Fudan University to study for a master's degree.

When I first came to China to study, my classmates came from all parts of the world and the campus just like "United Nations". Although I had visited many places in China, my Chinese was still awkward. At the beginning of studying abroad, the language became an obstacle. When I think of the difficulty of learning Chinese, I can't forget the embarrassing experience. One day, I went out to visit Beijing. When I got back to school, I was very tired, so I decided to take a taxi. At that time, I had been studying in BLCU for nearly a semester, and I felt that I could communicate in Chinese. After getting on the taxi, I told the driver, "I'm going to 'Bei Yu'." I felt that what I said is clear, but the driver didn't understand. I repeated it five times back and forth until I drew out the Chinese character of the school name. The driver suddenly realized: "Oh! 'Bei Yu'!" I kept muttering, didn't I say something like that? Later, I remembered that when speaking Chinese, one should pay attention to the tone. If the tone is wrong, the meaning may be different. Since then, whenever I speak, I pay special attention to the intonation.

With the help of my teacher and classmates, I have been learning Chinese smoothly and happily. The situation is not the same after the beginning of undergraduate study. There are few foreign students in the class. Most of the students are Chinese. The teachers gave lectures in chinese. The theoretical knowledge of international relations taught in Chinese was difficult for me to understand. Sometimes, some expressions the teacher used made Chinese students laugh. We, foreign students got total loss. Luckily my teachers and classmates were very nice and have helped us learn a lot. Since then, we have established profound friendship with Chinese friends. More and more exchanges, I have learned about Chinese society and civilization. With the deepening study of Chinese society, I began to participate in various activities inside and outside the school, and gained more friendship and some honors.

To sum up, I spent a quarter of my time in Beijing and Shanghai. During the years of studying in China, Chinese culture, politics, economy and all kinds of education had a profound influence on my production. I have not only felt the profound charm of the Chinese language, but also witnessed the rapid economic and social development of China in recent years.

After returning to Nepal after graduation, I have been engaged in the work related to China. I have become a Chinese teacher. I have taught undergraduate courses and Chinese studies. Now I am a Chinese lecturer at Confucius Institute, Kathmandu, Nepal. Based on the accumulation of teaching experience, in the past two years, I have started to work with Nepalese experts in China on the teaching, translation and research of Chinese and Nepalese languages. I have developed a lot of translation practice, published a lot of translated works, and also helped a number of cultural exchange activities. In ancient times, Xuan zang who went to the west to seek the true scriptures without fear of difficulties and dangers, and passed through Nepal, which opened the way for Sino Nepalese cultural exchanges. Today, a child who once could not even pronounce Tian'anmen Square, can represent his motherland Nepal with outstanding scholars from all over the world, to discuss how to become a young Sinologist who can make more contributions to the exchanges and cooperation between the two countries. This is the process in which my dream of "going east" has become true. China and Nepal have been friendly for generations. The two countries have a long history of cultural exchanges and have broad prospects for cooperative research. China is willing to share its development experience with us on the "Belt and Road" and jointly create harmonious development. I am willing to spare no effort to contribute to the cause of cultural exchange between the two countries.

“弃武从文”的汉语人生

［博茨瓦纳］马弈男

博茨瓦纳大学中文系讲师

我本来想安安静静地埋头做一位计算机系的老师，哪知被汉语迷住，从此“弃武从文”，开始了自己的汉语人生。

2017 年 3 月，我正式成为博茨瓦纳大学中文系的中文教师，给 4 个班

的学生讲课，课程排得很满。但我对自己说："我喜欢汉语，也喜欢去教学生怎样学习汉语，所以自己不觉得累，而是觉得很快乐。"

2009 年，我从博茨瓦纳大学计算机系本科毕业后，留校任助教，如按照正常的步骤，我今后会成为计算机系的教师甚至教授，一切的转折始于当年孔子学院的成立。

当年孔子学院正式在博茨瓦纳开始招生培训中文，教学点设在博茨瓦纳大学，每晚授课。我抱着试一试的态度去报名参加了培训班。当时我有好几个中国朋友，我想与他们及他们的家人有更深入的交流，所以想试试学习中文，看看自己能学到什么样的水平。

就是这一试，我发现自己的语言天赋竟然出奇地好。在孔子学院学习不到半年，老师们都说我的发音很准，对语言的掌握和运用也非常快，到学期结束时，中国驻博茨瓦纳大使前来向我们颁发证书，更让我感受到中国政府的友好。"就这样，我爱上了汉语，我想去中国，想把汉语学得更好。"我 2011 年申请了奖学金去湖南大学攻读计算机系的硕士。

我把湖南称作自己在中国的家乡，在湖南，我度过了最为忙碌的 3 年，也为今后的职业生涯转变奠定了基础。

在湖南读书期间，我一边忙着学习计算机课程，一边坚持学习汉语，有了语言环境，更是如鱼得水。

我的汉语水平突飞猛进，2013 年，我通过了汉语水平考试 HSK5 级考试（最高级为 6 级）。而这时面临着计算机专业的硕士学位论文写作，要拿出一篇合格的论文需要投入大量时间和精力。我意识到鱼和熊掌不可兼得，而随着对汉语的熟练掌握以及对汉语越来越浓厚的兴趣，我心中已逐渐明确了自己职业生涯的方向——要成为一名汉语教师。

我最终放弃了计算机系的学习，也就是切断了自己成为计算机系讲师这条业已成形的路。我于 2014 年考上上海师范大学，攻读汉语国际教育硕士，朝着专业汉语教师的方向努力，并于2016年7月顺利毕业。

我非常感谢上帝赐给我语言天赋，坚持不懈的学习和明确而坚定的方向给我的天赋插上一双隐形的翅膀，让我最终实现理想。

更何况这个理想已经有了可以生根发芽的土壤。与中国有多个合作项目的博茨瓦纳大学2011年就成立了中文系，非常需要汉语教师，我在此时选择汉语教学，可以说是恰逢其时，也赶上了中非友好的最好时期。

我对自己与中国的缘分感慨良多，我读小学的时候，我家的附近就有中国人在给我们修建中学，那时候我就很想听懂他们说的话，没有想到多年以后，还是中国政府给了我这样的机会，我真的很感谢中国。

我从中国学成回到博茨瓦纳就把自己当作中博关系的架桥人，我经常担任孔子学院活动、中博文化活动等的主持人，也积极参加中博关系的相关研讨活动等，生活中有博茨瓦纳朋友与中国人沟通遇到困难时也常求助于我。我希望通过自己，让更多的博茨瓦纳人了解中国，也让更多的中国人了解博茨瓦纳，增进相互之间的理解。

学习汉语让我展开了快乐而精彩的汉语人生，未来3—5年，我还计划去中国攻读博士学位，要把汉语教学的路踏实而坚定地走下去。我会珍惜去中国学习的机会，因为真的可以学到很多很多。

My Chinese Life Started from Chinese Language

Masule Gracious Tshepiso / Botswana

Chinese Department, Botswana University, Lecturer

I wanted to be a teacher in computer department quietly, but I was fascinated by Chinese and started my Chinese life.

In March 2017, I became a Chinese teacher of the Chinese Department in Botswana University. I had to give lectures to 4 classes. But I told myself, "I love Chinese, and I love teaching students how to learn Chinese, so I do not feel tired but very happy."

In 2009, when I graduated from the computer department of Botswana University, I left school as an assistant. If I follow the normal road, I will become a teacher and even a professor in the computer department. The establishment of Confucius Institute became the turning point.

In those days, Confucius Institute officially began recruiting and training Chinese in Botswana, and the teaching site was set up at Botswana University, where Chinese was taught every night. I took a try to sign up for the training class. At that time, I had several Chinese friends. I wanted to have deeper communication with them and their families, so I tried to learn Chinese and see what level I could learn.

It was this attempt that I found that my language talent was surprisingly good. Less than half a year after studying at Confucius Institute, teachers said that my pronunciation was accurate and I have mastered Chinese very quickly. By the end of the semester, China's ambassador to Botswana came to give us certificates, which made me feel the China government friendly. "In this way, I fell in love with Chinese. I want to go to China and learn Chinese better." In 2011, I applied for a scholarship to study for a master's degree in computer science at Hunan University.

I called Hunan in China my second hometown. In Hunan, I spent the most busy three years and made the foundation for the future career.

When I was studying in Hunan, I was busy learning computer courses, while insisting on learning Chinese. With the language environment, it was like a fish in the water.

My Chinese learning level has improved by leaps and bounds. In 2013, I passed HSK5 (the highest level is 6). At this time, I was preparing the computer master's degree thesis writing, but to take out a qualified paper needs to invest a lot of time and energy. I realized that fish and bear's paws can't be both, and with the mastery of Chinese and the growing interest in Chinese, I have gradually identified the direction of my career — to become a Chinese teacher.

I finally gave up the study of computer science, that is, I stopped the already formed road of becoming a computer department lecturer. He was admitted to Shanghai Normal University in 2014 and studied for a master's degree in Chinese international education. He worked hard to become a professional Chinese teacher and graduated successfully in July 2016.

I am very grateful for my gift of language, unremitting study and clear and firm direction, which give me a pair of invisible wings inserted in this talent, so that I can finally realize my ideal.

What's more, this ideal already has the soil which can take root and sprout. Botswana University, which has many cooperation projects with China, established the Department of Chinese in 2011. It needs Chinese teachers very much. I chose Chinese teaching at this time. It can be said that it was just in time and also caught up with the best period of Sino African friendship.

I feel a lot about my fate with China. When I was in primary school, there were Chinese people building a middle school for us near my home. At that time, I wanted to understand what they said. I didn't expect that the Chinese government would give me such an opportunity many years later. I really appreciate China.

When I returned from Botswana to learn from China, I regarded myself as the bridge erection of Sino Bo relations. I often served as a host of activities such as Confucius Institute activities, cultural activities in China and other places. I also actively participated in relevant research activities such as Sino Bo relations. In my life, Chinese friends did not understand the communication with Chinese people and often turned to him. I hope that through myself, more people in Botswana will understand Botswana. China has also enabled more Chinese people to understand Botswana and enhance mutual understanding.

Learning Chinese enabled me to have a happy and wonderful life. In the next three to five years, I plan to go to China to study for a doctor's degree, so as to make the road of Chinese teaching steady and firm. We really want to cherish the opportunity to study in China. We can really learn a lot.

做中国文化的传播者

［塞尔维亚］叶子
贝尔格莱德孔子学院秘书

我的中文名字叫叶子，我来自塞尔维亚西部的一个小城市。我是一个喜爱看书、听音乐、交朋友、有情有义、性格开朗的姑娘。

2007 年，我十分荣幸地成了贝尔格莱德语言大学中文系的新生。由于塞语和汉语之间存在巨大的区别，在刚开始学汉语的时候我遇到了不少困

难。但是我一直鼓励自己说，“坚持就是胜利嘛！再难也要坚持下去”。经过几年学习，我的知识慢慢积累、汉语也说得越来越流利。

2009 年，作为塞尔维亚代表团的成员之一，我参加了中国重庆市主办的第八届国际大学生汉语桥比赛。在中国的这两周时间虽然很短暂，但是对我来说非常重要。我当时真正地爱上了中国。我认识了很多中国朋友以及来自世界各地学习汉语的同学，初步体验了在中国生活是怎么样的。当时我下决心一定要再回到中国去。

大学毕业之后，我获得了汉语国际教育硕士奖学金。从 2011 年至 2013 年，我在中国传媒大学读过两年的研究生。当时对我影响最大的是书法课，书法不仅是一种艺术，而且也是一种享受生活的方式。我非常喜欢汉字，因为汉字有很深的文化内涵。我觉得这种世界上独一无二的文字所表达语义的方式非常巧妙，对我这个以拼音文字语言为母语的人来说，真的太神奇了！

目前我是贝尔格莱德大学语言学院的博士生。我的研究课题是通过龙的象征研究中国人民的文化与特性。希望通过此研究帮助大家更深刻地了解中国和中国文化。

我认为通过“一带一路”的项目可以促进塞尔维亚和中国之间友好关系，既可以使塞尔维亚人更好地了解中国，又可以使中国人对塞尔维亚加深了解和认识。

我觉得一个人首先要做好人。一个好人不仅要喜欢自己的职业，同时也应该明白知识是无穷无尽的，所以每个人也要不断地学习和发展。

20 世纪初，有一位传教士说过“您不应该问我中国怎么样，因为我已经离开中国三个月了，所以我介绍的中国及其人民可能只是它的过去。”每一年回中国的时候，我都感觉中国变化很大，但还是像回家一样。

老子说：“千里之行，始于足下。”

我对中国文化和人民的了解才刚刚起步。

To be an Introducer of Chinese Culture

Jelena Despotović / Serbia

Confucius Institute of Belgrade, Secretary

I'm Jelena Despotović and my Chinese name is Yezi. I come from a small city in Western Serbia. I like reading books, listening to music, making friends, I'm righteous, and have a cheerful personality.

In 2007, I was honored to be a freshman in the Chinese Department of Belgrade language university. Due to the huge difference between the two languages, I encountered a lot of difficulties at the beginning of learning Chinese. But I always encourage myself and say, "persistence is victory! No matter how difficult it is, I will stick to it." After several years of study, my knowledge has gradually expanded and my Chinese has become more and more fluent.

In 2009, as a member of the delegation of Serbia, I participated in the 8th International Chinese Bridge Competition for university students hosted in Chongqing, China. Two weeks in China are very short, but it is very important to me. I really fell in love with China. I have known many Chinese friends and classmates from all over the world who are learning Chinese. I have a preliminary experience of what life is like in China. At that time, I decided to go back to China.

After I graduated from University, I got a master's scholarship in Chinese international education. From 2011 to 2013, I was a graduate student in Communication University of China for two years. At that time, what influenced me most was calligraphy class. Calligraphy was not only an art, but also a way to enjoy life. I like Chinese characters very much because they have a deep cultural connotation. I think this unique word in the world expresses semantics in a very clever way. It's really amazing for me, who is a native language of Pinyin!

At present, I am a doctoral student in the language school of the University of Belgrade. The research topic is: To study the culture and characteristics of Chinese people through the symbol of dragon. It is hoped that this study will help you to understand China and Chinese culture more deeply.

China's one belt, one road project, I believe, can promote friendly relations between Serbia and China, which will enable Serbia people to better understand China and deepen Chinese understanding and understanding of Serbia.

I also think that everyone should be good first. A good man should not only like his career, but also understand that knowledge is endless, so everyone should constantly learn and develop.

At the beginning of the 20th century, a missionary said, "you should not ask me how China is, because I have been away from China for three months, so it may be a thing of the past for me to introduce China and its people." Every year when I go back to China, I feel that China has changed a lot, but it is still like going home.

Laozi said, "a journey of a thousand miles begins with one step."

My understanding of Chinese culture and people is still in its infancy.

我如何成长为一名汉语教师

［土耳其］法特玛
内夫谢希尔大学博士研究生、助教

2006 年，我考上了埃尔吉耶斯大学中文系。一听到我考上大学的消息，我就开心得不得了。中文专业在当时是一个很有前途的专业。现在还是一样。从小我就只有一个梦想，就是当老师。当什么老师不重要，只要是老师就行。高中的时候，我选了英文专业。老师们对我们说："好好学习。你们一定能考上英文系"。那时，我真的不知道我们也可以选其他语

言专业。我一直对大家说："我一定要考上英文专业。毕业以后，我就去纽约开一家书店"。青年人总是有各式各样的梦想，是不是？当时，我也是青年人。如果我能回到过去，我就对年轻的我说：你学习中文吧。中国那么大，中国人那么热情好客，中国文化真有意思，如果你考上中文系，你就一定会有美好的前途。我觉得当时年轻的我真的听到了我内心的渴望。我考上中文系以后，我的命运变得更好。我在埃尔吉耶斯大学中文系一年级的时候，我们系有两位中国老师，付老师和马老师。这两位老师在我大学生活中具有特殊的地位。付老师是一个充满热情的人，马老师讲课幽默，对我们要求也很严格。谢谢他们教我汉语。

在二年级的时候，在付老师的支持下，我参加了第七届"汉语桥"世界大学生中文比赛土耳其赛区比赛，得了第二名，获得了中国政府奖学金。奖金包括学费、住宿费及每个月的生活费。对我来说，这是一个难得的好机会，我不可能错过。因此，2008 年 8 月，我坐飞机去北京。这不仅是我经历第一次坐飞机，而且是我第一次出国。

到了北京，我非常惊讶！中国那么大！人多！车多！北京的地铁线也挺多的。在中国的生活，我有许多"第一次"的经历。比如：第一次坐地铁，第一次坐高铁，第一次跟外国人交流，第一次看京剧，第一次吃中国菜等。因此，来中国留学对我一生有很大影响。在北京语言大学学习汉语的过程中，我了解到中华优秀传统文化的丰富多彩。在北京，我参观了许多具有历史意义或特色的地方，比如，故宫、颐和园、长城、四合院、天安门、世界公园、798 艺术区、国家博物馆、鸟巢、动物园、海洋馆等。我在北京吃了好多好吃的菜。我是穆斯林，出国以前，我觉得在中国找不到清真菜馆。但真实的情况是，在中国的时候，我参观了许多城市并找到了许多清真餐厅。此外，在中国，各种宗教地位平等，和谐共处。中国十分尊重人们的宗教信仰。这使我内心平静、快乐！ 2009 年，在北京语言大学读完三年级后，我回国了。我在埃尔基耶斯大学继续读中文并于 2010 年毕业。当时，我参加并通过了中国政府的硕士奖学金考试，获得了硕士奖学金。2010 年 9 月，在东北师范大学开始读硕士。东北师范大学位于长春，最冷时能达到零下 35℃以下，外面冻死了！

在东北师大我的硕士专业是对外汉语。我的导师是黄晓赢教授。在我学习生活中，黄老师对我的帮助极大。学习和生活上，对外汉语专业的老师们和同学们也给我很大的帮助。在东北师大读硕士的时候，我不但充分了解自己，获取知识，也学习团队精神。因为有中国政府提供奖学金，我顺利完成了硕士学位学习。我要对中国政府表达真诚的感谢，感谢他们为我提供奖学金和学习机会。2012 年，我写完了论文并通过了硕士学位论文答辩。我的硕士论文题目是“土耳其学生运用汉语单音节趋向补语偏误分析及其教学对策研究”。2012 年 7 月 1 日，我获得了对外汉语硕士学位。2012 年 7 月末，我回国了。那时我并不想回国，但也没办法。因为我想当老师嘛！如果我不回国，就没有机会当老师了。2013 年 1 月末，欧凯老师给我打电话说：“内夫谢希尔·哈只·贝克塔·瓦里（Nevsehir Hacı Bektas Veli）大学创建了中国语言文学系，你想当助教的话，把所需的材料交给大学。”这是我人生中最快乐的时刻。我的梦想终于成真了。通过考试之后，我当上了助教。学校让我去安卡拉大学攻读博士学位。土耳其唯一的汉学教授欧凯教授是我的导师。感谢导师，选择了我。欧凯老师的专业是中国历史。因此，我也开始研究中国历史。我的博士论文题目是“郑和下西洋在中国历史上的地位”。2017 年 11 月 20 日，我通过了博士学位论文答辩。2018 年 1 月，我在内夫谢希尔·哈只·贝克塔·瓦里大学中文系正式开始工作。2006 年以来，我用心学习汉语，研究中国历史、文化、文学。我把悠久的中国历史文化教给学生。因为 2018 年是土耳其中国旅游年，我提前一年把土耳其尚勒乌尔法旅行宣传册及尚勒乌尔法旅游地图翻译成中文。2017 年，土耳其政府已决定土耳其各初中学校只要具备教学计划、教材和师资力量，即可开设汉语课程。2018 年 2 月，欧凯教授、我、艾图龙老师及其他学术委员会根据学生需求准备了教学计划。我希望土中共同努力加强两国关系。

我离开中国已经 6 年了。2014 年我跟我的同事艾图龙老师结婚。2015 年 9 月 15 日，我的儿子凯檑木出生了。我开始教他汉语。他学会了用汉语从“一”数到“十”。发音真标准！

我对中国有着特殊的感情。在我学习过程中，中国在我心中有特殊的地位。我非常热爱中国，中国是我的第二个故乡。

How Do I Grow to be a Chinese Teacher

Fatma Ecem Ceylan / Turkey

Nevsehir Haci Bektas Veli, PhD Student, Assistant

In 2006, I was admitted to the Chinese Department of Erciyes University. As soon as I heard that I was admitted to university, I was very happy. Chinese was a promising major at that time. It's still the same now. Since I was a child, I have only one dream, that is to be a teacher. It doesn't matter what subject to teach, just be a teacher. In high school, I chose English as my major. The teachers all said to us, "study hard. You must be admitted to the English department." That is, I really don't know that we can also choose other language majors. I have always said to you: "I must be admitted to English major." After graduation, I went to New York to open a bookstore. Young people always have all kinds of dreams, don't they? At that time, I was also a young man. If I can go back to the past, I will say to the young me: you learn Chinese. China is so big. The Chinese are so hospitable. Chinese culture is really interesting. If you enter the Chinese Department, you will have a bright future. But I think I really heard my inner wish when I was young. After I was admitted to the Chinese Department, my destiny became better. When I was a freshman in the Chinese Department of Elgies University, there were two Chinese teachers in our department. They are Mr. Fu and Mr. Ma. They occupy a special position in my college life. Mr. Fu is a person full of enthusiasm. Mr. Ma is humorous and strict with us. I feel very thankful for their teaching me Chinese.

In the second grade, with the support of Mr. Fu, I participated in the final of the 7th "Chinese Bridge" world university students Chinese competition in Turkey, and won the second place and the Chinese government scholarship. The full award includes tuition, accommodation and monthly living expenses. For me, this is a rare opportunity. I can't miss it. Therefore, in August 2008, I flew to Beijing. This is not only my first flight experience, but also my first overseas experience.

When I arrived in Beijing, I was very surprised! China is so big! There are so many people! Lots of cars! There are also many subway lines in Beijing. In the process of living in China, there are many "first-time" experiences. For example, I took the subway for the first time, took the high-speed rail for the first time, communicated with foreigners for the first time, watched Beijing opera for the first time, and ate Chinese food for the first time. Therefore, studying in China has a great impact on my life. In the process of learning Chinese at Beijing Language and Culture University, I understand the rich and colorful Chinese excellent traditional culture. I visited historic places in Beijing. For example, the Forbidden City, the Summer Palace, the Great Wall, the quadrangle, Tian'anmen Square, the World park, 798 Art District, the National Museum, the bird's nest, zoo, aquarium, etc. And I ate a lot of delicious food in Beijing. I am a Muslim. Before going abroad, I don't think we can find halal food in China. However, when I was in China, I visited many cities and found many halal restaurants. In addition, in China, all religions have equal status and coexist harmoniously. China respects different religions very much. This makes me happy! After finishing my third year in Beijing Language and Culture University, I returned to China in 2009. I continued to study Chinese at elkyres University. Graduated in 2010. At that time, I took part in the master's scholarship examination of the Chinese government. Passed the examination and won the master's scholarship. In September 2010, I began to study for a master's degree in Northeast Normal University. Northeast Normal University is located in Changchun. When it is coldest, it can reach below -35℃. It's freezing outside!

My major is Chinese as a foreign language. My tutor is Professor Huang Xiaoying. In my study life, Mr. Huang helped me a lot. In my study and life,

TCFL teachers and students also give me a lot of help. When I was a master in Northeast Normal University, I not only fully understood myself, acquired knowledge, but also studied team spirit. Thanks to the scholarship provided by the Chinese government, I completed my master's degree. I would like to express my sincere thanks to the Chinese government for providing scholarships and learning opportunities. In 2012, I finished my thesis and passed the defense of master's degree thesis. The title of my master's thesis is "Turkish students using monosyllabic directional complement error analysis and teaching countermeasures". At the end of July 2012, I returned home. That is, I don't want to leave China, but I have to. Because I want to be a teacher. If I don't come back home, I won't have a chance. At the end of January 2013, Mr. o'kai called me and said, "Nevsehir Hac ı bektas veli university founded the Department of Chinese language and literature. If you want to be an assistant, give the materials you need to the University. This is the happiest moment of my life. My dream finally came true. After passing the exam, I became a teaching assistant. The school asked me to go to Ankara University for a doctorate. The only Sinology professor in Turkey, Professor Oukai, is my tutor. Thank you for choosing me. Oukai's major is Chinese history. Therefore, I also began to study Chinese history. The title of my doctoral thesis is "the position of Zheng He's voyages to the West in Chinese history". On November 20, 2017, I get my doctorate.

In January 2018, I started working in the Chinese Department of Nevsehir Hac ı bektas veli University. Since 2006, I have studied Chinese history, culture and literature. I teach students the long history and culture of China. Because 2018 is the year of Chinese tourism in Turkey, in 2017, I translated the brochure of Turkey and the tourist map of shangle urfa into Chinese. In the same year, the Turkish government has decided that all junior high schools in Turkey can offer Chinese language courses as long as they have teaching plans, teaching materials and teachers. In February 2018, Professor o'kai, I, Dr. Fatma, Mr. arturon and other academic committees have provided teaching plans according to the needs of students. I hope Turkey and China will make joint efforts to strengthen bilateral relations.

It has been six years since I left China. In 2014, I married my colleague,

Mr. arturon. On September 15, 2015, my son kaishimu was born. This year, I began to teach him Chinese. He learned to count from one to ten in Chinese. What a standard pronunciation!

I have special feelings for China. I love China very much and China is my second hometown.

我与中国 23 年的缘分

［韩国］文有美
延世大学讲师

我和中国的缘分已有 23 年了。可以说我人生中的一半以上时间是和“中国”一起度过的。为了写这篇“我的中国故事”，我也回顾了我和中国的这 23 年。

一个高中生和中国

从我上高中的时候选择主修中文开始，我第一次接触到了中文。也是在那时，我结识了第一位中国朋友——当时还与我校有着姐妹学校关系的北京四中学生，我们成了笔友，通过信件交流。

为了本次写作我重新翻出20年前的信件，这让我激动不已。虽然上了大学之后我们失去了联系，但是她作为我的第一个中国朋友，给我留下了一段美好的回忆。

一个大学生和中国

我深深地喜欢上了“中文”，所以选择大学专业的时候也是义无反顾地选择了中文专业。之后，我用自己两年打工攒下来的钱，首次踏上了中文研修之路——那是2001年2月，去北京语言大学上语言（汉语）研修班。

在韩国学习中文的时候，我曾经努力过，也曾有过自信。但是到了北京之后才发现自己的不足，特别让我苦恼的是北京人的“儿化音”。

但是在语言研修过程中，我第一次接触到了来自世界各国的朋友和他们一起旅行的时光至今让我念念不忘。

第一次去的旅游地是大同，是我生平去过的旅游景点当中最好的一处。特别是在山海关看日出的场景，至今令我难以忘怀。

遗憾的是，由于非典疫情，我不得不中断研修提早回国，没能圆满完成我的研修课程。

一个博士生和中国

我一直难以忘怀语言研修的中途告退。在2010年，我终于重新开始了自己的“汉语语法”课程——那是在上海复旦大学攻读博士学位的课程。我在中国攻读博士所积累的经验是无法用金钱来衡量的。我还记得那难忘的一幕幕。

场景一：语法沙龙

语法沙龙的师兄、师姐、师弟、师妹们是和我一起度过快乐时光的伙伴。和他们在一起时，我可以敞开心怀，就像一家人一样。和他们在一起时，其乐融融，无拘无束，自由自在。

场景二：春游

每当春秋到来之际，指导老师戴耀晶会组织游学。令我至今难忘的一次春游是井冈山大学游，也是最后一次游学。当我看着那张大家都穿着由我亲手制作的 T 恤衫的合影时，不由地会流出眼泪来。因为 2014 年，我的指导老师戴耀晶教授因病去世了。

中国的留学生活，不仅帮助我增长知识，也极大地帮助我加深对中国文化的理解。因为我可以跟中国朋友一起学习，一起生活，从中体会到真正的中国人的生活。

现在的我和中国

现在我仍在从事与中国相关的工作。我的家人也都喜欢中国，并且经常一起去旅行。2017 年夏天，我们一家人去成都旅游，孩子们也在那里学习了汉语。

目前，我在学习汉语语法，并且通过汉语授课来挣钱。人们说，如果把喜欢的事情当作职业，就不能从中感受到乐趣。但是我想坚持说，（研究）自己最喜欢的汉语，就能从中找到真正的价值和乐趣。

通过这次机会，我发现我的人生和“中国”是息息相关的。

China and I Together for 23 years

You Mi Moon / South korea
Yonsei University, Lecturer

China and I have been together for 23 years. It can be said that more than half of my life is spent with China. In order to write this "My China story", I also review the 23 years that belong to me and China.

A high school student and China

When I was in high school, I chose to major in Chinese, and I got to know Chinese for the first time. At that time, I met my first Chinese friend. At that time, the students of Beijing NO.4 middle school, who also had a sister school relationship with our school, became pen pals and communicated through letters.

For the sake of this writing, I turn over the letters from 20 years ago, which makes me feel the intersection. Although I lost contact after I went to university, she left me some good memories as my first Chinese friend.

A college student and China

I am deeply in love with "Chinese", so when I choose university major, I also choose Chinese major without hesitation. After that, I used the money I had saved from working for two years and embarked on the road of Chinese study for the first time. In February 2001, I went to Beijing Language and Culture University to study Chinese.

When I studied Chinese in Korea, I had tried hard and had confidence. But after I arrived in Beijing, I found my own shortcomings. What bothered me most was the "Er Hua sound" of Beijingers.

But in the process of language training, I met friends from all over the world for the first time, and the time of traveling with them still makes me remember.

Datong, the first scenic spot I visited, is one of the best scenic spots I have ever visited. Especially in Shanhaiguan to see the sunrise scene, so far let me unforgettable.

Unfortunately, due to the SARS epidemic, I had to interrupt my study schedule and return home early. I failed to finish my course successfully.

A doctoral student and China

I can't forget the end of my language study. Finally, in 2010, I started my own "Chinese grammar" course again. It was a doctoral program at Fudan University in Shanghai. When I was studying for a Ph.D. program in China, the experience I gained could not be measured in terms of money. I still remember that unforgettable scene.

Scene 1: grammar Salon

The senior brothers, sisters, younger brothers and sisters of grammar salon are my partners to spend a happy time with me. When I'm with them, I can open up, just like a family. When we are with them, we are happy, free and free.

Scene 2: spring outing

When the spring and Autumn period comes, Dai Yaojing, the instructor, will organize a study tour. My unforgettable spring outing is Jinggangshan tour and the last one. When I look at the photo of everyone wearing a T-shirt made by me, I can't help but cry for my instructor, Professor Dai Yaojing, passed away in 2014.

Studying abroad in China has not only helped me in my knowledge, but also in my understanding of Chinese culture. That's because I can learn and live with Chinese friends and experience the real life of Chinese people.

China and me now

Now I'm still working with China. My family also like China and often travel together. Last summer, my family went to Chengdu for a tour, and the children also learned Chinese there.

At present, I'm learning Chinese grammar and making money by teaching Chinese. People say that if you take something you like as a career, you can't enjoy it. But I want to continue to speak (Research) my favorite Chinese and find real value and fun from it.

Through this opportunity, I found that my life and "China" are closely related.

一位汉语教师的成长

［白俄罗斯］习滢

明斯克国立语言大学教师

2015 年，我从明斯克国立语言大学毕业。我所学的专业是语言学，毕业后教授英语和汉语。学习外语不仅是我的爱好，也是我的职业。我从 10 岁就开始学英语了，所以我能说一口流利的英语。2012 年我开始学习中

文，这一选择彻底改变了我的生活。学中文给了我很多好处。首先，现在我能说世界上最流行的语言了。第二，学习汉语激发了我对独特的中国文化的兴趣，我学得越多，就感到越有趣。第三，它开阔了我的视野，开阔了我的世界观。

其中对我最大的机遇是明斯克国立语言大学孔子学院提供的来中国学习汉语的机会。在中国黑龙江大学的这一年，是我一生中最难忘的经历。首先，让我有机会与母语人士交流，提高我的语言技能，这对一名汉语教师来说非常重要；其次，我遇到了很多来自世界各地的优秀人士，他们分享了自己的经验，给了我很多帮助，成了我真正的好朋友；第三，我了解了很多中国文化和传统。我参观了北京、上海、南京、曲阜等中国著名的城市，这都帮助我更好地了解中国人，了解他们的文化、价值观、传统和习惯。

如果没有学习这个国家的文化、人民和他们的生活方式，学习这个国家的语言就不可能是完整的。这就是为什么我非常感谢这样一个机会。

我在明斯克的一所综合性学校当了一年的汉语教师。这是一次非常有意义的经历，因为和孩子们一起工作有助于我掌握教学和提高交流技巧。现在我很荣幸成为明斯克国立语言大学的一名汉语教师。与别人分享自己的知识和经验，激发他们学习中国语言和文化的兴趣，激发他们学习和发现更多的东西的感觉很棒。我想把汉语教学作为自己的事业，这就是为什么我想继续在中国学习。这将有助于我提高我的汉语水平，因为现在我还有许多不足之处。在我看来，要想教别人，首先要自己成为一名专业人士。这就是为什么我怀着感激之情接受一切机会去中国提高我的专业技能。

The Growth of a Chinese Teacher from Belarus

Buldyk Natallia / Belarus
Minsk State Linguistic University, Teacher

In 2015 I graduated from Minsk State Linguistic University. My major is linguistics, teaching English and Chinese. Learning foreign languages is not only my hobby but also my profession. I have been studying English since I was 10, so I can speak it fluently. In 2012 I started learning Chinese and this event changed my life completely. Learning the Chinese language has given me a lot of benefits. Firstly, now I am able to speak the most popular language in the world. Secondly, learning Chinese arouses my interest in unique Chinese culture, and the more I learn, the more interesting it gets. And, thirdly, it broadens my horizons, my worldview.

One of the most valuable benefits was the opportunity to learn Chinese in China, given by the Confucius Institute in Minsk State Linguistic University. This very year in China, in Heilongjiang University, was the most unforgettable experience in my life. First of all, it gave me the opportunity to communicate with native speakers and to improve my language skills, which is very important for me as a teacher of Chinese. Secondly, I met a lot of wonderful people from all over the world, who shared their experience, helped me a lot and became really good friends for me. Thirdly, I learned much more about China, Chinese people, Chinese culture and traditions. I visited great famous places in China like Beijing, Shanghai, Nanjing, Qufu etc. It helped me better understand Chinese people, their culture, values, traditions and habits.

Learning a foreign language cannot be complete without learning the culture of the country, its people and their lifestyle. That is why I am very grateful for such an opportunity. And I hope there will be more of them in future.

I have worked as a teacher of Chinese in one of the comprehensive schools in Minsk for about a year. It is a really useful experience, because working with children helped to master my teaching and communicative skills. Now I am a Chinese teacher in Minsk State Linguistic University, and it is an honor for me. It is great to share one's knowledge and experience with other people, to arouse their interest in learning the Chinese language and culture, to inspire them to learn and discover more. I would really like to make my career in teaching Chinese that is why I want to continue study in China. It will help me to improve my acquisition of Chinese. In my opinion, in order to teach other people one should become a professional himself first. That is why I accept with gratitude all the opportunities to go to China to improve my professional skills.

了解中国，介绍中国

［巴西］丁小雨

里约热内卢大学澳门国际学院博士候选人、皇家图书馆研究员

我叫丁小雨，具有巴西和美国国籍，我的母亲是巴西人，父亲是华裔美国人，我于1986年12月15日出生在里约热内卢。我是巴西里约热内卢州立大学艺术史与批评的博士研究生。我在巴黎狄德罗大学获得艺术、美学和比较文学硕士学位，在法国巴黎索邦大学获得艺术史和考古学学士学位。

我正在进行的研究是有关中国和葡萄牙文化交流中的东方艺术品收

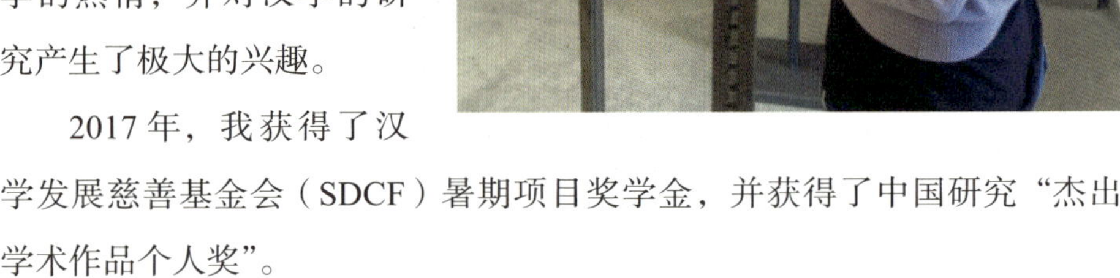

藏。该项目由澳门国际学院（International Institute of Macau）与位于里约的葡萄牙皇家阅读内阁（Royal Portuguese Reading Cabinet）合作提供的奖学金。

2016年，我获得了里约热内卢天主教大学孔子学院提供的在中国河北大学学习一个月的奖学金。在那里，我发现自己对汉学的热情，并对汉学的研究产生了极大的兴趣。

2017年，我获得了汉学发展慈善基金会（SDCF）暑期项目奖学金，并获得了中国研究“杰出学术作品个人奖”。

我在获得汉学发展慈善基金会奖学金期间所从事的工作是一次重要的经历，我的研究使我更好地理解中国哲学。我有机会参加并聆听中国著名学者的讲座，认识了这些教授。

同样，青年汉学家访学计划对我的研究也非常重要，因为我沉浸在中国新的学术环境中。这是一个吸收新的观点很好的机会，我还能将所学内容应用到我的研究和讲座中。

艺术和语言也是我人生中的两大爱好。艺术对我来说一直以来也是一种语言，把我和其他对艺术有热情的人联系起来。我曾是罗浮宫博物馆的文案专家，圣彼得堡俄罗斯艺术学院的实习生，美国巴黎基金会的常驻画家以及美国国家美术学院的学生。

事实上，我的中国血统（来自上海）让我产生了一种与我的传统重新融合的愿望。

我的专业目标是加深我对中国文化的理解，为我的研究奠定坚实的基础并将中国介绍给我的学生。青年汉学家研修计划刚好提供这个机会来丰富和发展我的计划。

Knowing China, Introducing China

Caroline Pires Ting / Brazil

Macau International College, Rio de Janeiro State University, Ph. D. candidate; Royal Library, Researcher Fellow

My name is Caroline Pires Ting (丁小雨), I am a citizen of Brazil and USA, born to a Brazilian mother and a Chinese-American father, in Rio de Janeiro, on December 15th, 1986. I am a Ph.D. candidate in Art History and Criticism at the State University of Rio de Janeiro, Brazil. I hold an M.A. in Arts, Aesthetics and Comparative Literature at the University of Paris-Diderot and a B.A. in Art History and Archeology at the University of Panthéon-Sorbonne, France.

My ongoing research regards collecting Oriental Art in the cultural interaction between China and Portugal. This project blossomed from a scholarship granted by the International Institute of Macau, in partnership with the Royal Portuguese Reading Cabinet in Rio, highlighting Chinese and Lusitanian intercultural dialogue.

In 2016, I received a scholarship to study a month at the Hebei University, China, offered by the Confucius Institute at Pontifical Catholic University of Rio de Janeiro (PUC-Rio). There, I developed my passion for Sinology and became extremely interested in pursuing research on it.

In 2017, I received a scholarship from the Sinological Development Charitable Foundation (SDCF) for its summer program and got the "Individual Prize for Outstanding Academic Work" in China Studies.

The work I undertook during my scholarship granted by the SDCF was an important experience and my research called for a better understanding of Chinese philosophy. I had the opportunity to attend lectures by renowned Chinese scholars and get acquainted with these professors.

Likewise, the Visiting Program for Young Sinologists will be very important to my research, given the immersion in new academic settings in China. It will be a rewarding opportunity to assimilate new perspectives and to apply the learned content into my research and lectures.

Arts and languages are also two long-life passions of mine. Art has always been a sort of language for me, connecting me to everyone else who possesses an enthusiasm for it. I have been a copyist at the Louvre Museum, a trainee at the Russian Academy of Arts in Saint Petersburg, an artist-in-residence at the American Foundation of Paris, and a student at the National Academy of Fine Arts (USA).

As a matter of fact, my own Chinese origin (from Shanghai) has created in me a desire to reconnect with my heritage.

My professional goal is to deepen my understanding of Chinese culture and acquire a solid foundation to pursue my research and introduce China to my students. The Visiting Program for Young Sinologists will provide an opportunity to enrich and develop my projects.

我学习汉语的故事

［菲律宾］洪秀萍

亚太进步之路基金会研究分析员、暨南大学国际关系学院博士研究生

从我五岁起中国语言和文化就自然而然地走进了我的生活，那时我去了菲律宾的一所中国学校，亚虞山培青中学（Timber City Academy）。除了教授中文课程和庆祝中国节日外，亚虞山培青中学还为我提供了与菲律宾华人社区交流的机会，也使我理解了在菲律宾的华人族群特点。

高中时，我与菲律宾华文学校的学生一起参加了厦门华侨大学的暑期游学夏令营。我在厦门的那段经历改变了我的人生，不仅仅是沉浸在中文的教育和文化中，这也是我第一次离家。对我来说一开始并

不容易，我必须了解拼音的用法，因为在学校的学习中，注音只被用作学习普通话的工具。但是令人欣慰的是，我和我的同学们可以和福建当地人交谈，话在菲律宾也很普遍。直到今天，这个夏令营始终在帮助学生进一步练习标准汉语和福建方言。

曾经令人愉快的学习经历、让人着迷的中国语言和文化，现在促成了我对国际关系的兴趣。这些年来，我对中国的兴趣越来越浓，还获得了国际关系专业硕士学位。目前我正在从事研究工作，主要研究菲中关系。两国关系最近发生的变化以及中国在地区和全球舞台上的作用，使研究这一问题更加令人兴奋。此外，我的区域研究还包括“一带一路”倡议和菲律宾外交政策。

我过去的经历使我相信，人与人之间的交流可以增进理解、确定合作领域。青年汉学家研修计划必将成为我的“中国故事”中一段难忘的经历。在这样的学术交流环境中，我希望通过同汉学家、东道主大学和项目委员会的讨论，加深学术话语和相互尊重的意识。我期待着在整个项目中聆听精彩的讲座，分享与会专家的见解，参加有意义的活动。

My Story of Learning Chinese Language

Grace Guiang / Philippines

Asian-Pacific Progress Foundation, Research Analyst; PhD Student, School of International Studies, Jinan University

Chinese language and culture seemed to naturally come into my life. It began when I was five, mainly because I went to a Chinese school, Timber City Academy (亚虞山培青中学), in the Philippines. Aside from Chinese-taught subjects and celebrating Chinese holidays, TCA opened opportunities that enabled me to mingle with the Filipino-Chinese community; in a long term I acquired an understanding of their ethnicity in the country.

In high school, I participated in a summer study-tour camp at Huaqiao University (华侨大学) in Xiamen with students from Filipino-Chinese schools. My stay in Xiamen was truly a life-changing experience—other than educational and cultural immersion, it was my first time to be away from home. It was not easy at first as I had to catch up with the use of *Pīnyīn* (拼音), because all years in school *Zhùyīn* (注音) was used as a learning tool for Mandarin. On the other hand, it was comforting that my fellow students and I can converse with the locals in Fujian, which is also widely used in the Philippines. This annual camp continues to allow students to further practice standard Chinese and Fujian dialect until today.

What used to be pleasant studies and appreciation on Chinese language and culture turned into an interest in international relations. Through the years, my interest in China developed and not surprisingly led me to take master's degree in International Studies. Currently I am pursuing research as a career, focusing on Philippines-China relations. The recent turnaround of events in their relations and the role of China in regional and global stage just made studying it more exciting. Moreover, my area studies also include the Belt and Road Initiative and Philippine foreign policy.

Based on my encounters in the past, I believe people-to-people exchanges can develop understanding and identify areas of cooperation. The Visiting Program for Young Sinologists will definitely bring another unforgettable milestone to my Chinese story. An environment for scholarly interaction, it is my hope that the fellowship will deepen the sense of academic discourse and mutual respect through the discussions among fellow Sinologists, the host university, and the program Committee. I look forward for substantial lectures, sharing of insights, meaningful engagements throughout the program.

将中国文学作品翻译到缅甸

［缅甸］杜光民
自由职业者（翻译家）

诺贝尔文学奖得主莫言在瑞典学院发表的文学演讲的主题是：“讲故事的人”。用他自己的话说，他是“因为讲故事得了诺贝尔文学奖”的。著名作家余华也曾经这样说过，“我从事的工作是讲故事”。他们两位都擅长讲故事，而我则是将我读过并喜欢的故事翻译给缅甸的读者阅读。在

此，我也来讲一讲“我的中国故事”。

首先自我介绍一下，我的名字是 Kaung Min，中文名是杜光民。我来自缅甸，从事文学翻译工作，就是将优秀的中国文学作品翻译给缅甸读者阅读。我是医学院毕业的，但我从小非常喜欢福尔摩斯侦探小说，并羡慕其作者柯南·道尔，所以，我梦想长大以后要像他一样既做医生也是作家，于是走上了文学这条路。其实，中国伟大的文学家鲁迅先生也是学过医的；还有孙中山先生，他更是学过医、行过医的伟大的革命家、政治家。本来想要成为一个作家的我，现在已经成为一名文学翻译者。我从 2008 年开始出版自己的译作。

2015 年夏天，我第一次来到中国，是到北京领奖。那一年，我获得“中华图书特殊贡献奖青年成就奖”。“中华图书特殊贡献奖”是中国的国家级对外文化奖项，旨在表彰在向海外介绍中国、推广中国文化和中国出版物等方面做出突出贡献的外籍及外裔华人作家、翻译家和出版家。“青年成就奖”是在该奖项成立十周年时设立的奖项。我是以青年翻译家的身份获奖的。

那一次北京之行，我有机会认识到来自世界各地的翻译家、汉学家。2017 年我第二次来北京，有机会参观北京国际图书博览会。这一次，我是去参加中外文学出版翻译研修班的，有一个礼拜的时间，所以认识了更多的朋友。最让我感动的是，我能够见到莫言老师本人，并能与他对话。至今，我已经在缅甸翻译并出版莫言老师的三部长篇小说——《蛙》、《生死疲劳》和《红高粱家族》。我最近也开始翻译余华老师的一些作品。他的代表作《活着》的缅文版 2018 年在缅甸出版。另外，2017 年，我不仅见到了莫言老师，而且还和其他翻译家们一起去拜会了余华老师。我们一起喝茶交流。那一次的茶会，真是令人难忘。

到过几次中国之后，我比以前更喜欢喝茶了。虽然没来中国之前，我也几乎每天都喝茶，但那只是“喝”茶，而不是“品”茶。我现在开始试着去品尝各种各样的茶。品一壶好茶，看一部好书，然后将这本书里写的故事翻译给读者阅读，那不是一件很快乐的事情吗？

接下来的几年里，我将会继续品尝各种各样的好茶，阅读各种各样的好书，然后将自己读过并喜欢的中文图书翻译给缅甸读者阅读。

Translating Chinese Literature into Myanmar

Kaung Min / Myanmar

Freelance (translator)

The theme of Mo Yan's literary speech delivered at the Swedish Academy is "storyteller". In his own words, he won the Nobel Prize in literature for telling stories. Yu Hua, a famous writer, once said, "my job is to tell stories.". Both of them are good at telling stories, and I translate stories I have read and like to Myanmar readers. Here, I would also like to tell you my Chinese story.

First of all, let me introduce myself. My name is Kaung Min, and my Chinese name is 杜光民 . I come from Myanmar, engaged in literary translation, that is to translate excellent Chinese literary works to Myanmar readers. I graduated from medical school, but I was very fond of Sherlock Holmes detective stories when I was young, and envied its author Conan Doyle. Therefore, I dreamed that I would be a doctor and a writer like him when I grew up, so I embarked on the road of literature. In fact, the great Chinese writer, Mr. Lv Xun, also studied medicine, and Dr. Sun Yat Sen was a great revolutionary and statesman who had studied and practiced medicine. I wanted to be a writer, but now I have become a literary translator. I started publishing my own translation in 2008.

In the summer of 2015, I came to China for the first time. I went to Beijing to receive the award. In that year, I won the "China Book Special Contribution Award youth Achievement Award". "Chinese books special contribution award" is China's National Foreign Culture Award. It aims to recognize foreign and overseas Chinese writers, translators and publishers who have made outstanding contributions in introducing China to overseas countries, promoting Chinese culture and Chinese publications. The "youth Achievement Award" is established on the 10th anniversary of the award. I won the prize as a young translator.

On that trip to Beijing, I had the opportunity to meet translators, sinologists and teachers from all over the world. Two years later, in 2017, I came to Beijing for the second time and had the opportunity to visit the Beijing International Book Fair. This time, I went to attend the Chinese and Foreign Literature Publishing translation seminar. I had a week, so I got to know more friends. What moved me most was that I could see Mr. Mo Yan himself and have a dialogue with him. Up to now, I have translated and published three novels of teacher Mo Yan in Myanmar — "frog", "life and death fatigue" and "Red Sorghum family". I also began to translate some works of Mr. Yu Hua recently. The Burmese version of his masterpiece alive was published in Myanmar in 2018. In addition, I not only met with Mr. Mo Yan in 2017, but also had the opportunity to visit Mr. Yu Hua with other translators. Let's have tea together. The tea party was unforgettable.

After several trips to China, I like tea more than before. Although I had been drinking tea almost every day before I came to China, it was just "drinking" tea, not "tasting" tea. I'm now trying to taste all kinds of tea. Isn't it a very happy thing to taste a pot of tea, read a good book, and then translate the story written in the book to the readers?

In the next few years, I will continue to taste all kinds of good tea, read all kinds of good books, and then translate the Chinese books I have read and like to Myanmar readers.

雪·京剧·中国画

［印尼］林雪莹
雅加达建国大学中文系主任

1998 年 8 月 18 日，我第一次来北京是到北京语言大学留学。

我在印尼本科读的是中文系，从零起点开始学习汉语。对我来说，汉语很难学，能够掌握好汉语不是一件简单的事情。大学毕业时，我意识到自己的汉语不流利（也有人说我五音不全，洋腔洋调），感觉自己大学 4 年的汉语学习没有学好，便想到中国留学。得到父母和姐姐的支持后，我就下决心去北京深造。其实，我原本想报读艺术学院学习中国国画，因为我很欣赏国画，也很欣赏中国书法。没想到，因为当年印尼暴乱，报名到中国留学的学生太多，所以老师将我的报名表弄错了。我本来填报的是北京语言大学艺术学院，结果被录取在该校语言学院。

人算不如天算。既然收到录取通知书，那我就去学习语言吧！虽然有点失望，但是我自我安慰：到了北京还有机会学习国画。只要有机会，我学习国画的梦想还能实现。

到北京的第一天，我发现气温跟印尼相差太大。北京当时快到秋天了，而我来自热带国家，一下子不能适应。我本来就怕冷，所以有点难受。朋友建议我去五道口买秋衣。穿上秋衣，身体感到暖和多了。身体感

觉舒服后，也就有精神学习了。

在语言学院学习汉语期间，我过得很快乐。与我一起留学的同学们来自世界各国。我能用汉语跟其他国家的同学交流，很有成就感，也更加有信心。几乎每天下午，我都在学校的球场上跟北京的老百姓打乒乓球，不仅提高了打乒乓球的水平，同时也提高了汉语表达能力。运动能热身，同时能交新朋友。当时，北京没有空气污染，秋天的空气非常新鲜，所以，我感觉在北京生活比在印尼生活更健康。

11 月底的一天清晨，我睁开眼睛向窗外望去，看到棉花似的东西从天上掉下来。我兴奋地告诉同屋室友，下雪了。室友是韩国留学生，她见多不怪，继续入睡。而我是第一次看到下雪，不想错过这个机会，于是，马上穿好衣服，跑去找朋友一起堆雪人、打雪球。整个校园铺满白雪，非常壮观。这时，我什么烦恼都没有了。雪下得越大，我们玩得越兴奋。玩累了，我们就躺在雪上聊天，做白日梦。

过了一个学期，我的汉语进步很快。当中央电视台招募留学生参加京剧比赛时，我便自告奋勇地报了名。我喜欢挑战，好奇心很强。以前，我只是在电视里看到京剧，但根本听不懂演员们到底在唱什么。对我来说，有机会学习京剧，尤其是中央电视台派专业老师给参赛者进行一个月的培训，是非常难得的机会，我一定要抓住。

初学京剧，非常辛苦。首先得张开嘴巴，好像吃块石头似的，让声音从肚子里发出来。然后得学习弯腰，还要学拉脚拖腿的慢步走法。老师教

我唱京剧大师梅兰芳的“天女散花”：“云外的须弥山色空四显，毕钵岩下觉岸无边。大鹏负日把神翅展，迦陵仙鸟舞蹁跹。八部天龙金光闪，又见那入海的蛟螭在那浪中潜，阎浮提界苍茫现，青山一发普陀岩。”老师让我边唱边跳，把感情表达在歌词和动作上。这时，我感觉自己就是天女。尤其是比赛那天，我被打扮成京剧旦角儿，连自己都认不出自己来了。可惜在舞台上，当我看到观众和评委时有些紧张，歌词忘了，不过动作都记得一清二楚。我只能跳、走，不能唱。虽然我比赛没有获奖，但感到很满足，自己体会到学习京剧的可贵之处。对我来说，学习京剧的经验是无价之宝。

第二年，我有机会在艺术学院学习国画，我的梦想终于实现了。这种喜悦，只能意会无法言传。2000 年 2 月，我开始学习工笔画和中国书法。在老师的指导下，我画了不少画。我最喜欢自己画的工笔画，其中有两幅还参加了展览。我也学会了在印章上雕刻自己的名字。

在北京学习的时间一眨眼就过去了。虽然我很喜欢北京，但我毕竟是印尼人，还得回国。临回国那一天，我与学校的老师和朋友依依不舍。我想如果有机会再来北京，我一定会去看望老师。同学们都各奔东西了，但老师永远住在北京。没有老师也没有今天的我。

Snow · Peking Opera · Chinese Painting

Liem Yi Ying / Indonesia

Chinese Department, Binus University, Jakarta, Dean

On August 18, 1998, my first visit to Beijing was to study in Beijing Language and Culture University.

I studied Chinese as an undergraduate in Indonesia and began to learn Chinese from scratch. For me, Chinese is very difficult to learn. It is not a simple thing to master Chinese well. When I graduated from University, I realized that I was not fluent in Chinese (some people said that I was not perfect in five tones and foreign accent). I felt that I had not learned Chinese well in four years of college, so I wanted to study in China. After getting the support of my parents and sister, I decided to go to Beijing for further study. In fact, I wanted to apply to the art college to study Chinese painting, because I appreciate Chinese painting and calligraphy. Unexpectedly, because of the riots in Indonesia, too many students signed up to study in China, so the teacher made a mistake in my application form. I originally filled in the art school of Beijing Language and Culture University, but I was admitted to the school of language.

It's better to calculate by man than by heaven. Now that I have received the admission notice, I will learn the language! Although I was a little disappointed, I comforted myself that I still had the opportunity to learn Chinese painting in Beijing. As long as I have the chance, my dream of learning Chinese painting can be realized.

On my first day in Beijing, I found that the temperature was too different from Indonesia. Beijing was about to fall, and I came from a tropical country and couldn't adapt to it. I'm afraid of the cold, so I feel a little uncomfortable. My friend suggested that I go to Wudaokou to buy autumn clothes. Put on autumn clothes, the body feels much warmer. When you feel comfortable, you will learn mentally.

I had a good time studying Chinese in the language institute. The students I studied with came from all over the world. I can use Chinese to communicate with students from other countries. I feel very successful and confident. Almost every afternoon, I play table tennis with the people in Beijing on the school court, which not only improves the level of playing table tennis, but also improves the ability of Chinese expression. Exercise can warm up and make new friends. At that time, there was no air pollution in Beijing, and the air in autumn was very fresh, so I felt that living in Beijing was healthier than living in Indonesia.

One morning at the end of November, I opened my eyes and looked out of the window to see something like cotton falling from the sky. I excitedly told my roommate that it was snowing. My roommate is a Korean student. She keeps sleeping. And it was the first time I saw snow, and I didn't want to miss this opportunity. So I immediately put on my clothes and ran to find friends to make snowmen and play snowballs. The whole campus is covered with snow, which is very spectacular. At this time, I have nothing to worry about. The more snow fell, the more excited we were. Tired of playing, we lie on the snow chatting, daydreaming.

After a semester, my Chinese improved very fast. When CCTV recruited foreign students to take part in the Beijing Opera Competition, I volunteered. I like challenges and I'm curious. Before, I only saw Peking Opera on TV, but I couldn't understand what the actors were singing. For me, it's a good thing to have a chance to learn Peking Opera, especially when CCTV sends professional teachers to train the contestants for one month. I must seize the rare opportunity.

It's very hard to learn Peking Opera. First of all, you have to open your mouth, like eating a stone, and let the sound come from your stomach. Then you have to learn to bend down and walk slowly. My teacher taught me how to sing

Peking Opera master Mei Lanfang's "Heavenly Maids Scatter Blossoms": "Xumi mountain beyond the clouds is full of color, and the river is boundless under the Bibo rock. The giant ROC spreads his wings in the sun, and the fairy birds of Jialing dance lightly. The eight heavenly dragons glittered with gold, and the dragon that went into the sea was diving in the waves. Yan futi's boundary was boundless, and the green mountain was just like Putuo rock. " The teacher asked me to sing and dance, expressing my feelings in lyrics and movements. At this time, I feel like I am the goddess of heaven. Especially on the day of the competition, I was dressed as a Beijing Opera Dan actor, and I couldn't even recognize myself. Unfortunately, on the stage, when I saw the audience and the judges, I was a little nervous. I forgot the lyrics, but I remember the movements clearly. I can only dance and walk, not sing. Although I didn't win the prize in the competition, I felt very satisfied and realized the value of learning Beijing opera. For me, the experience of learning Peking Opera is priceless.

The next year, I had the opportunity to study Chinese painting in the art college, and my dream finally came true. This joy can only be expressed in words. I began to learn meticulous painting and Chinese calligraphy in February 2000. Under the guidance of the teacher, I drew a lot of pictures. I like my own meticulous paintings best, and two of them have also been participated in the exhibition. I also learned to carve my name on the seal.

The time of studying in Beijing passed in the blink of an eye. Although I like Beijing very much, I am Indonesian after all and have to go back home. On the day of returning home, I was reluctant to part with my school teachers and friends. I think if I have a chance to go to Beijing again, I will certainly visit my teacher. The students are all on their own, but the teacher lives in Beijing forever. No teacher, no me today.

做中印文化交流的使者

[印度]黎明

古吉拉特中央大学中文助理教授

印度和中国是世界上两个文明古国，有着3000多年的悠久历史，文化交流极为丰富。正如印度总理纳伦德拉·莫迪最近在与习近平主席举行非正式会谈时所说的："两国共同构成了世界经济的50%，而另外50%则被世界其他国家分享了1600年。"我们注意到这两个国家过去的辉煌和潜在的能力。中国是丝绸和瓷器的生产国，而印度是棉花和香料的生产国。印度是连接东方中华帝国和西方罗马帝国的古代丝绸之路的重要地点和参与者。在印度古典名著《摩诃婆罗多》和考提利亚的《政事论》中，人们可以发现丝绸分别被称为 chinanshuk 和 chinipatta，前缀“chin”强调了丝绸的中国起源。佛教进一步连接和加强了两个文化丰富和多元的国家之间的关系。法显、玄奘、义净三位高僧前往印度追求佛经和经文。7 世纪玄奘的印度之行，仍然在两国的双边关系中创造着凝聚力。在世界著名的古代纳兰达大学遗址上修建了玄奘纪念堂，人们至今仍对这位高僧的来访记忆犹新。他以《大唐西域志》的形式所做的叙述，在印度的研究中也同样重要，考古学家一直在用它来填补印度历史上的某些空白。

印度的僧侣，如卡萨帕·玛坦加（Kasyapa Matanga）和达摩拉塔（Dharmaratna）等到中国传播佛教教义的贡献至今仍被人们铭记，现代有印度总理曾于 2010 年在洛阳白马寺为巨型雁塔落成致辞。

中国著名的学者季羡林认为孙悟空是印度猴神哈努曼的代表。

明代伟大的航海家郑和曾多次访问印度南部的港口城市，如卡利卡特、科钦、科尔兰、哥印拜陀等。在印度语中，糖被称为“**चीनी**-Chini”，这表明制糖技术是从中国传入印度的。类似的还有渔网，花生（chiniyabadaam），说明这些都是从中国舶来之物。

殖民时期，印度和中国都遭受殖民帝国的剥削、歧视，使两国走上了共同命运的道路。印度独立和中华人民共和国成立后，两国在 1954 年共同接受了和平共处五项原则，在外交上为世界和平与和谐指明了道路。在印地语把这一时期称为中印亲如兄弟（Chini BhaiBhai）的时代。在短暂的边界争端和小规模冲突之后，双方在邓小平和拉吉夫·甘地的领导下再次建交。

中国除了是印度最大的邻国外，在印度人民的心目中，她一直是拥有灿烂的神秘传统文化的国度。

在学习汉语之前，我对中国的了解是通过不同的功夫电影。在印度，商贩们生产和销售中国食品，这些食品的名称与中国人的名字很像，比如 Chowmin，Momo，但是味道很印度。大多数人听说中国，都会想到功夫电影、面条和佛教，这些画面很快就会在脑海中浮现。但现在，中国经济的发展更加引人注目，中国有勤劳的人民和世界工厂，繁华的城市如上海、深圳拥有世界一流的基础设施和动车网络。

我的中国故事始于 2003 年。当时我被新德里尼赫鲁大学中国和东南亚研究中心录取使我有机会学习这门奇妙的语言。这次机会永远改变了我的生活。我第一次接触这个中文词，当然是“你好”，那是武汉大学中文系的王志远教授教给我的，当时他是尼赫鲁大学的客座教授。我在那里学习中文，取得了学士学位，在攻读硕士学位的同时，2007—2008 学年我以交换生的身份获得了北京外国语大学的奖学金，这对我来说就像是梦想成真。2007 年 8 月 29 日，我来到了中国的首都北京，机场当时新的 3 号航站楼没有投入使用。我看到人们都在全神贯注地工作，中国乘客匆匆地去赶他们的航班，去迎接他们的家人。我还没见过这么多中国人，这对我来说是一个全新的世界。我从机场出来，遇到了从大学来接我的司机。他给我的印象不一样，衣着整洁，举止得体，非常专业（他的自我介绍让我很惊讶，后来我才知道，中国司机的工资相对来说很高）。

我放眼北京的大街，环路——当时最外面是五环路，六环路在造。我们的车正驶向我们的大学，沿途看到了高楼大厦，许多大型购物中心，各种品牌的豪华轿车，在当时的印度公路上我很难找到这些。因此，这次中国之行给我的第一印象是一个先进的现代中国。

从那以后，我去过中国很多次，去过很多城市。我也有机会参加 2010 年印度青年访华代表团，并参观了上海世博会。中国最显著的变化是一线、二线和三线城市基础设施的空白被迅速填补，只是沿海和内陆城市的一些差异。现在，中国已经在全国建立了先进的高速列车网络。上次我去的时候，我有机会乘高铁从北京到无锡旅游。许多发展中国家不得不向中国学习。

五年前我开始在印度中央古吉拉特大学教授中国语言和文化。从一个学习汉语的学生到成为一名汉语教师，这是一段难忘的“旅程”。我还主动协助与中国不同大学签订谅解备忘录，以促进两国学术和教育的相互交流，并在我国总理 2016 年访问中国时在两国重要领导的见证下，与暨南大学和中国北京外国语大学签署了谅解备忘录。

印度和中国都是世界上增长最快的两个发展中国家，可以说是现代世界经济增长的引擎。印度和中国是世界上最大的两个市场，人口占世界总人口的 36% 以上。没有访问过中国的印度人和没有访问过印度的中国人对彼此有很多误解。他们不了解实际情况，包括文化遗产、经济活动、社会政治进步、传统和习俗等。更多的人与人之间的接触，学者之间的交流，电影和其他流行文化的交流都是增进了解的途径。像我这样支持印度与中国关系的支持者完全赞同习近平主席提出的双边关系观，即作为两个最大的发展中国家和人口超过十亿的新兴的经济体，中国和印度是世界多极化和经济全球化的支柱。

我相信我的中国故事和印中故事是分不开的。而且，我希望在未来继续努力，为这两个亚洲国家 26 亿多人民宣传和参与充满活力、双赢的印中故事。

To be a Messenger of the Cultural Exchanges between China and India

Prabhat Kumar / India

Gujarat Central University, Assistant Professor of Chinese

India and China are two ancient civilizations of the world which have glorious history of more than 3000 years of immensely rich and cultural exchanges. As Indian Prime Minister Narendra Modi in recently concluded informal meeting with President Xi Jinping said "the two countries together constituted for about 50 per cent of the world economy and another 50 per cent was shared by rest of the world for 1600 years", drew our attention on glorious past and hidden capabilities in these two country. China was producer of silk and porcelain, whereas India was of cotton and spices. India was an important place and player of ancient silk route which connected Chinese empire in east to Roman empire in the west. One can find the mention of silk in Indian classic Mahabharata (摩诃婆罗多) and Kautilya's (考底利耶) Arthashastra (政事论) as chinanshuk and chinipatta respectively, the prefix "chin-" underscoring its Chinese origin. Buddhism further connects and strengthens the relationship of two culturally rich and diverse countries with each other. Three great monks Fa Xian (法显), XuanZang (玄奘), Yi Jing (义净) travelled to India in pursue of Buddhist sutras and texts. XuanZang and his journey to India during 7th century is still creating cohesive strength in the bilateral relationship of these two countries. XuanZang Memorial Hall built at the site of world famous ancient Nalanda University, still refreshes the memory of visit of this great monk. His narratives in the form of famous book "*Great Tang Records on the Western Regions*" (《大唐西域记》) also has equal importance in the studies of India, and archaeologists have been using it to fill in certain gaps in Indian history.

Indian monks such as Kasyapa Matanga and Dharmaratna as well as their contributions who went to china to spread the teachings of Buddhism are still remembered, temple of White horse in Luo Yang (洛阳白马寺) inaugurated by Indian President in 2010 and Giant Wild Goose Pagoda (大雁塔) are its live example.

Famous Chinese Indologist Ji Xianlin considered Sun Wukong as representation of Indian monkey god Hanuman.

The great admiral of Ming dynasty Zheng He (郑和) several times visited many southern port cities of India such as Calicut, Cochin, Kollam, Coimbatore during his naval voyages. As in hindi sugar is called as "चीनी-Chini", it suggests sugar-making technology arrived in India from China. Similarly fish catching net, peanut (花生 -chiniyabadaam) all paved their way from China.

During Colonial period, India and china both faced exploitation, discrimination in the hand of colonial empire, which brought these two together in the fate/path of common destiny. After independence of India and liberation of china, both jointly accepted the Five Principal of Peaceful Coexistence in 1954 and showed the path for peaceful and harmonious world in the diplomacy. There was era of Hindi-Chini BhaiBhai (中印亲如兄弟). After brief border disputes and skirmishes, both again engaged in diplomatic ties under the leadership of Deng Xiaoping and Rajiv Gandhi.

Besides being the largest neighboring country of India, in the eye of Indian people, China is all along a place of glorious mystic traditional culture.

Before starting study of Chinese language, I have known china through various Kong Fu movies. There are various vendors making and selling Chinese foods which have resemblance of Chinese names such as Chowmin, Momo, but Indianised taste. Most of the people when listen about china, it was the Kong Fu movies, noodles and Buddhism which instantly comes as image in the mind earlier. But now, it is the eye-catching economic development, bustling city of Shanghai, Shenzhen with world class infrastructures, one of the largest networks of the bullet trains, hard working nature of people and the world's factory.

My China Story started when I got the chance to study this fantastic language in the year of 2003 when I got the admission in the Centre for Chinese & South East Asian Studies of Jawaharlal Nehru University, New Delhi. And, it changed my life forever. My first encounter with the Chinese word was, of course, Ni hao (你 好) and the Chinese person was Professor Wang Zhiyuan of Chinese department of Wuhan University who was as a visiting professor in Jawaharlal Nehru University at that time. I studied Chinese there, completed my B.A. and while doing my Master, I got the scholarship as exchange student to study Chinese in Beijing Foreign Studies University of China in academic year 2007-08, it was like dream came true for me. I landed in Beijing—the capital of largest country of the east on 29th August, 2007. At the airport, at that time new terminal 3 was not operational. I could see Chinese people attentively working here and there, Chinese passengers hurriedly running in and out to catch their flights, to meet their family members who had come to receive them. I had not seen such a huge number of Chinese at a same time earlier, it was a new world for me. I came out from the airport, and met the driver who had come from the university to receive me. He gave me a different impression, neatly dressed, well behaved, very professional (actually I was really amazed by his presentation, latter on I came to know that drivers in China have a very handsome salary comparatively).

I was on the street of Beijing, ring road, at that time outer most was the 5th ring road and 6th was in making. Our vehicle was heading towards our university, saw high rise buildings, many big shopping malls, big and luxurious cars of different brands on road, which I was difficult to find on Indian roads at that time. So, the first impression which got in Beijing was of an advanced modern China.

Since then, I have gone to China many times and travelled many cities. I have also got opportunity to participate in Indian Youth Delegation to china in the year of 2010 and visited World Expo in Shanghai. The most remarkable change is that China has rapidly filled the gap in basic infrastructures of first tier, second tier and third tier cities, except some differences of coastal and inland cities. Now, China has built up an advanced network of Bullet trains all over the country. Last time when I visited, I had opportunity to travel from Beijing to Wuxi. Many developing countries have to learn from china.

I began to teach Chinese language and culture at Central University of Gujrat in India last five years ago. It is a memorable journey from a student of Chinese language to becoming teacher of the Chinese language. I also took initiative to have MoU between our University and different Chinese Universities to promote mutual academic and educational exchanges between two countries, as a result of it our university signed MoUs with Jinan University and Beijing Foreign Studies University of China in the presence of Education minister of China and the honorable President of our country India when he visited China in the year of 2016.

Although, Chinese proportion and contribution in to current world economy in comparison to India, is huge, but India and China both are two fastest growing developing countries of the world, we can say that the engine of growth of modern world economy. With more than 36% of the world population jointly, India and China are the two biggest markets of the world. Indian who did not visit china and Chinese who didn't visit India are having many misconceptions about each other. They are not aware of real situations including cultural heritages, economic engagements, socio-political advancements, traditions and customs. More people to people contacts, exchanges of academicians and scholars, exchanges in cinema and other popular cultures are ways to enhance understanding. The supporter of better India-China relations like me fully agree with the President Xi Jinping's view of bilateral relationship that as the two largest developing countries and emerging-market economies with a population level of more than one billion, China and India are the backbone of the world's multi-polarization and economic globalization.

I believe my China story is not separated from the India-China story. And, I want to work hard continuously in future to promote and be a part of India-China story which is vibrant in nature, and win-win for more than 2.6 billion people of these two Asian nations.

以我之笔　写中国故事

［英国］月雪芳
自由职业者（配音演员、作家、翻译家）

中国对我来说是一片遥远的土地，一个散发着神秘色彩的地方。直到有一天一切都变了……

现在我在写一部小说，故事发生在广东省、云南省和苏格兰一个叫克雷尔的小渔村之间。我一直对中国很好奇，但直到2009年我在南非罗德大学（Rhodes University）时，我才决定进一步研究中国。我很快就喜欢上了汉语，并决定参加汉语桥比赛。最终我获得了孔子学院奖学金并继续在暨南大学学习。

从那时起，我发现自己不断地被中国吸引，在过去的十年里，我大部分时间都在深圳为一家中国最大的创意和文化公司工作。我被汉字以及每个汉字都能讲述一个故事的方式所吸引。我在台湾师范大学学习了一年的繁体字，并获得奖学金在台湾各地研究创意艺术。

作为演员和作家，我对讲故事的艺术以及这种艺术可以采取的不同形式非常感兴趣。当我住在深圳的时候，我与人共同创建了一个名为“深圳故事”的组织，这个组织为人们提供了一个平台，大家可以在这里分享故事。我还参与了爱丁堡深圳创意交流会，这是中国和苏格兰之间极好的一次合作。

我正在创作的小说中有个中国角色因为要学习粤剧从云南来到了广州。为此我开始研究岭南文化，同时很高兴有机会在广东进一步探索和研究岭南文化。

我相信，当代中国可以通过传统的讲故事形式——主要是评书、歌剧、图画讲故事、民歌和诗歌——为世界其他地区激发创造性，成为文化催化剂。在写我的小说时，我的目的是强调这一点，特别是因为这是一部当代小说，但人物仍然对古老的、传统的中国艺术形式感兴趣。这表明，即使在我们不断取得进步和实现现代化的过程中，传统文化仍然是迷人的和鼓舞人心的，因为人们总是在寻找自己的根。怀旧在这里也扮演着重要的角色，因为今天的许多年轻人渴望过一种更简单的生活并渴望“穿越”回古代去体验他们祖先成长的传统。

中国拥有丰富的创造力，而这往往因为它的技术进步和商业影响力被忽视。然而，不可否认，一个社会的源头是其非物质文化遗产。这就是我们发掘中国丰富文化的独特之处，我希望通过我对中国的写作来强调这一点。

在写小说的同时，我也在写一系列双语儿童读物，想要打破人们对中国的成见。我想向人们展示是什么让中国如此令人惊叹并突出中国文化中让我着迷的部分。我还将创立一个播客，关注中国的创意。

我非常期待再次来到中国，通过我在广东的研究，我希望能写一篇关于保护和弘扬中国传统文化艺术的重要性的研究论文，同时也希望加深我对中国非物质文化遗产的认识，使我的小说更加真实，来源于第一手的研究。

我真的相信是命运，缘分把中国带进了我的生活，我对即将到来的挑战感到兴奋。总会有更多有趣的事情要我去发现，我已经等不及了。

Writing Novels With Chinese Background

Siobhan Lumsden / United Kingdom

Freelancer (dubber, writer, translator)

China was always a distant land to me, a faraway place that exuded mystery. That was until one fateful day when everything changed...

Now here I am, researching and writing a fictional novel set between Guangdong province, Yunnan province and a small fishing village in Scotland called Crail. I have always been curious about China, but it was only in 2009 when I was at Rhodes University in South Africa that I decided to pursue it further. I very quickly fell in love with the language and decided to compete in the Chinese Bridge competition, whereby I was granted a Confucius Institute Scholarship to continue my studies at Jinan University in Guangzhou.

Since then I have found myself being continually drawn back to China and I spent the better part of the past decade working for one of China's biggest creative and cultural companies in Shenzhen. I am fascinated by the written language and the way that every character almost tells a story. I spent a year studying traditional Chinese characters at National Taiwan Normal University, and was also awarded a scholarship to research creative arts around Taiwan.

As an actor and writer, I am extremely passionate about the art of storytelling and the different forms that this can take. When I lived in Shenzhen I co-founded an organisation called Shenzhen Stories which provides a platform for people to come together as a community and share stories. I was also very involved with the Edinburgh Shenzhen Creative Exchange which is a fantastic collaboration between China and Scotland.

In the novel I am writing, one of the Chinese characters moves from Yunnan to Guangzhou to embark on her quest to learn Cantonese opera. I am therefore researching Lingnan Culture, and am so grateful to have the opportunity to explore and research this further in Guangdong.

I believe that contemporary China can act as a creative and cultural catalyst for the rest of the world through the use of its traditional storytelling forms-mainly its pingshu, opera, pictorial storytelling, folk songs and poetry. In writing my novel I aim to highlight this, especially as it is a contemporary novel but still the characters are intrigued by the older, more traditional Chinese art forms. This shows that even as we progress and modernise, traditional culture will always be fascinating and inspiring because people will always be seeking to explore their roots. Nostalgia also plays a huge part here, as many of today's youth aspire to live a more simple life and with this comes a desire to traverse the traditions their ancestors grew up with.

China has an abundance of creativity, and this is often overlooked in favour of its technological advancements and its business influence. However, there is no denying that the source of a society is its intangible cultural heritage. That's where we get to unearth what makes China's rich culture so unique, and I am committed to highlighting this through my writing about China.

At the same time as writing my novel, I am also working on a series of bilingual children's books that aim to breakdown preconceived ideas or stereotypical notions that people may have about China. I want to show people what makes China so amazing, and highlight the parts of Chinese culture that led me to fall in love with it. I will also be starting a podcast that is focused on creativity in China.

I am very much looking forward to being in China again and from my research in Guangdong, I hope to put together a research paper on the importance of preserving and promoting traditional Chinese culture and arts both within China and abroad, as well as furthering my insight into Chinese Intangible Cultural Heritage so that my novel will be more authentic and stem from firsthand research.

I really believe that it was fate, the Chinese "Yuanfen" that brought China into my life, and I am excited about the adventure that lies ahead. There will always be something more to discover and I cannot wait for what's next in my lifelong relationship with China.

好奇·学习·了解

［越南］陈灯忠

越南河内国家大学讲师

我小时候第一次通过电影接触中国文化。孙悟空的故事和他西天取经的故事吸引了我，为一个渴望冒险和探索的年轻人打开了一个神奇的世界。《三国演义》中引人入胜的人物形象，使我对中国人的忠贞、忠心、聪明才智等产生了敬仰，对自己希望给社会带来和平与和谐的理想产生了感悟。在一个小男孩的眼里，中国是一个具有不可抗拒的吸引力的地方，一个有着伟大传统和人民的国家。

我怀着成为人文学者的抱负长大并花了很多时间阅读我国的历史和文学，意识到我们越南人如果不了解中国文明，就无法真正了解自己。就像欧洲人对希腊和罗马的感激一样，我们的祖先通过学习中国的模式和生活方式来建立一个独立的国家。我们效仿了中国的语言、教育和官僚体系，但保留了我们的文化、主权和坚韧精神。

作为一名大学生，我有机会更深入地了解中国文化。我被文言文的美和书法艺术迷住了。每个汉字都有自己的故事和意义，可以追溯到几千年前。《诗经》中的诗歌以一种朴素而优雅的方式反映了人的情感。读李白，犹如登高远眺，高瞻远瞩，而杜甫的作品则向我们展示了世人的悲剧和苦难。中国的历史教会了我如何认识人，如何知道王朝的兴衰，如何在挑战和艰辛面前保持冷静和谦虚，如何在这个动荡的世界中找到一条出路并保持一种平静的心态。我被中华文明的广度和深度所折服。

我很荣幸能参加 2018 年青年汉学家研修计划（广州）。对我来说，这是一次深入了解中国的宝贵机会。作为一名青年汉学家，我真的希望我能帮助促进我的国家和中国之间的相互了解与合作，与世界各地的朋友分享我对中国文化的热爱，并将我通过这个项目获得的知识传播给我的学生。

Curiosity · Learning · Knowing

Tran Dang Trung / Vietnam

College of Humanities and Social Sciences of Vietnam National University, Hanoi, Lecturer

I first encountered with Chinese culture through television films when I was little. The story of Sun Wukong and his journey to the West captivated my imagination, opened up a whole wonderful world to a young mind yearning for adventure and exploration. The fascinating characters in *Romance of Three Kingdoms* made me admire the Chinese values of faithfulness, devotion, and cleverness, appreciate the ideal of bringing peace and harmony to the society. In the eyes of a young boy, China was a place of irresistible attraction, a country with great tradition and people.

Growing up with the ambition of becoming a scholar in humanities, I have spent time reading more about my country's history and literature and realized that we, the Vietnamese, could not really understand ourselves without knowing about Chinese civilization. Like the European being indebted to the Greek and Roman, our ancestors have acquired the Chinese model and way of life to create an independent nation. We imitated the Chinese language, education, and bureaucracy but preserved our culture, sovereignty, and spirit of resilience.

As a university student, I had an opportunity to learn more deeply about Chinese culture. I was mesmerized by the beauty of classical Chinese and the art of calligraphy. Each Chinese character has their own story and meaning which can be traced back thousands years ago. The poems in *Shijing* reverberates the feelings and emotions of human beings in a simple but very elegant way. Reading Li Bai is like flying atop mountains to see the world in an elevated perspective while Du Fu's works show us the tragedies and sufferings of common people on earth. The history of China taught me how to understand human beings, how to know about the rise and fall of dynasties, how to be calm and humble in front of challenges and hardships, and how to find a way and a mentality in this turbulent universe. I was overwhelmed by the scope and range and the greatness of Chinese civilization. And I have a dream to know more about China, more about the tradition that I inherited.

It is my privilege to be accepted to the 2018 Visiting Program for Young Sinologists (Guangzhou). This gives me a precious chance to fulfill my aspiration to know more about China. As a young Sinologist, I really hope I could help to promote the mutual understanding and cooperation between my country and China, to share my love of Chinese culture with friends from all over the world, and to spread my knowledge acquired through the program to my students.

从“偶然”到“必然”

［韩国］柳多絮
前成均中国研究所助理研究员、北京大学政府管理学院博士研究生

韩国有句俗语：“如果‘偶然’出现了三次，就是‘必然’。”当初收到征集“我的中国故事”这一邀请的时候，我偶然想起这句话。我与中国的缘分，从哪里开始的呢？坐在咖啡厅，细细一想，往事历历在目。从很久以前的事情到最近的，我脑子里有许许多多跟中国有关的记忆，其中有三段最为强烈。我想，正是这三段难忘记忆让我与中国的缘分成为“必然”。

我与中国最初的缘分跟《三国演义》有关。韩国有句话说，“如果不读《三国演义》三遍，那你就很难融入社会。”这句话的意思就是《三国演义》收罗很多生活的智慧、野心、背叛、爱情等。小学时期，我每周末跟妈妈一起去图书馆。某天，妈妈对我说了这句话，并往我的手里塞了一本《三国演义》。当然那时我还很小，所以妈妈给我的不是成年人读的《三国演义》，而是 60 本一套的漫画书。虽然当时我看的是漫画书，但是周围很多大人都称赞我，所以我感到非常骄傲，并且慢慢喜欢上《三国演义》。《三国演义》中给我最深刻的印象是“包子”的由来，而且，我从那个时候开始一直到现在，最喜欢的食物是包子。可是，《三国演义》说这包子就是诸葛亮首创的！当时我想，虽然在地理上中国与韩国距离很近，但是在文化上没有太密切的联系。因为那个时候的我还很小，并不知道中国与韩国在文化方面有那么密切的渊源，所以，《三国演义》中关于包子的故事让我很吃惊。从那时起，我认识到中国与我已经有密切的关联。

我与中国的另一段缘分是大学时期的一门中国政治课。2010 年，我读大学本科的时候，修读了一门《中国政治论》课。这门课第一次让我萌生以中国为研究对象。大学时期，关于“民主果真是没有代替方案的最好体制吗”，我的确是存有疑问的。这就是说，如果选举是既合理又有效的方法，为何整个社会没有广泛使用？作为投票行为者的公民为何不能总是做出合理性的选择？然而 2010 年第一学期，我在修读《中国政治论》这门课时，学习到与韩国的民主体制相比不一样的、有“中国特色”的独特政治体制，其中对政治改革和“中国特色”的民主讨论尤其感兴趣。通过这门课，我第一次听到与西方式“民主”（democracy）相比不同的中国式“民主”概念，从而打破过去对民主框架的理解，扩大了自己认识的范围。由此，我在学习的过程中第一次体验到心潮澎湃，被中国政治迷住了。后来，我对中国的独特发展方向与内在活力产生更大的好奇心，希望能够深入研究，所以就攻读了硕士学位。

我与中国的第三段缘分是一次中国之旅。2013 年，我在读研究生时一个人前往中国，开启从威海到香港的旅游。此次旅行，我不仅亲眼看见、亲身感受中国各地的环境与文化，而且感觉到对中国及中国人的亲近感。从威海到北京 15 个小时晚班列车的经历，我印象尤其深刻。当时，我虽然已进入研究生院，但是尚未决定选择以中国为研究对象，所以还没有学习汉语，而且一句汉语也不能说。在那种情况下，我的导师与父母却推荐我到中国旅行。我首先抵达的城市是靠近韩国的威海。威海当地的一位中国朋友为我做向导，让我顺利结束当地的旅行。下一个旅游地点是北京。我决定乘晚上的火车前往。韩国的领土比中国小很多，火车的运输时间很短，我以前没有坐卧铺车的经验，所以这个晚上的火车旅行对我是新的挑战。另外，因为我不能说汉语，所以我的朋友非常担心我的旅程。我乘坐的火车晚上 9 点出发，所以当我到达火车站时，天很黑。我买的票是硬卧车的中铺，火车夜晚需要关灯，加之语言不通，所以在火车上我感到非常恐怖，不能睡觉。天亮之后，我洗漱回来，突然有位阿姨跟我搭话。我们俩用英语聊天，气氛亲切温柔。这时，我才放心，并感受到中国人深刻的情意。我怀着无比喜悦的心情到达北京。那天的记忆至今仍然留在我的心中。

与中国的三段缘分，是我人生中非常难忘的记忆，可以说是刻骨铭心。与中国的三段缘分，使我“必然”选择中国作为研究对象。真是应验了那句俗语：“如果‘偶然’出现了三次，就是‘必然’。”虽然现在我还非常年轻，未来的发展也有很多不确定因素，但有一点可以肯定，我想把学习中国文化、研究中国作为自己未来一个重要的努力方向。我想，这也许就是我命运中的“必然”。

From Accidental to Inevitable

You Dasom / South Korea
Institute for Chinese Studies, Sungkyun, Former Assistant Researcher;
PhD Student, School of Government, Peking University

There is a Korean saying: "if accidental appears three times, it is inevitable." When I received the theme of "my Chinese story", I came up with this sentence. Where did my fate with China begin? Sitting in a coffee shop, I can remember the past. From the events of a long time ago to the recent events, I have a variety of memories related to China in my mind, three of which are the most powerful. I think it is these three strong memories that make my fate with China inevitable.

My first relationship with China is related to the *Romance of the Three Kingdoms*. There is a saying, "if someone doesn't read the *Romance of the Three Kingdoms* three times, don't have a dialogue." *The Romance of the Three Kingdoms* contains a lot of wisdom, ambition, betrayal, love and so on. In primary school, I went to the library with my mother every weekend. One day, my mother said this to me, and put a Book of *Romance of the Three Kingdoms* into my empty hand. Of course, I was still very young at that time, so what my mother gave me was not the *romance of the Three Kingdoms* read by adults, but a set of 60 comic books. Although I was reading comic books at that time, many adults around me praised me, so I felt very proud and gradually fell in love with the *Romance of the Three Kingdoms*. In the *Romance of the Three Kingdoms*, the most impressive thing for me is the origin of "baozi". Moreover, from then on, my favorite food is baozi. However, "Romance of the Three Kingdoms" said that this steamed stuffed bun was created by Zhuge Liang! At that time, I thought that although China and South Korea are very close geographically, they are not very closely related culturally. Because I was very young at that time, I didn't know that China and South Korea had such close cultural ties, I was shocked by the story of baozi in the *romance of the Three Kingdoms*. From this time, I realized for the first time that China and I have a close relationship.

Another fate I had with China was a Chinese politics course in college. In 2010, when I was an undergraduate, I took a course of Chinese politics. This course is the first time that I started to study China. When I was in college, I really had doubts about "is democracy really the best system without any alternative scheme?". That is to say, if election is a reasonable and good method, why is it not widely used in the whole society? Why can't citizens, as voters, always make reasonable choices? However, in the first semester of 2010, during the course of "on Chinese politics", I learned a unique political system with "Chinese characteristics" and a positive political history of China, which is different from the democratic system of South Korea. I was particularly interested in political reform and democratic discussion with "Chinese characteristics". Through this course, I heard for the first time the concept of "democracy" in Chinese style, which is different from that in western style, thus breaking the past understanding of the framework of democracy and expanding the scope of my understanding. Thus, in the process of learning, I experienced for the first time the surge of emotion and was fascinated by Chinese politics. Later, I became more curious about China's unique development direction and internal vitality, hoping to further study, so I studied for a master's degree.

My third predestination with China is a trip to China. In 2013, when I was a graduate student, I went to China alone and started a tour from Weihai to Hong Kong. During this trip, I not only witnessed and experienced the environment and culture of China, but also felt a deep sense of closeness to China and the Chinese people. I was particularly impressed by the 15 hour evening train from Weihai to Beijing. At that time, although I had entered graduate school, I had not yet decided to choose China as the research object, so I had not yet learned

Chinese, and I could not speak a word of Chinese. In that case, my tutor and parents recommended me to travel to China, so I decided to travel to China. The first city I arrived at was Weihai, near South Korea. A local Chinese friend in Weihai served as a guide for me to finish my trip successfully. The next place to visit is Beijing. I decided to take the evening train. I don't have a lot of train travel experience in South Korea, so I don't have much train travel experience in China. Besides, because I can't speak Chinese, my friends very worry about my journey. The train I took that night started at 9 p.m., so when I got to the station, it was very dark. The ticket I bought is the middle berth of the hard sleeper. The train needs to turn off the lights at night. In addition, I don't know the language, so I feel terrible on the train and can't sleep. After daybreak, I came back from washing, and suddenly an aunt spoke to me. The two of us chatted in English in a friendly and gentle atmosphere. At this time, I felt relieved and felt the deep affection of the Chinese people. I arrived in Beijing with great joy. The memory of that day is still in my heart.

My three predestination with China is a very deep memory in my life, which can be said to be unforgettable. Three times of predestination with China made me "inevitably" choose China as the research object. It really fulfills the saying: "if 'by chance' appears three times, it is 'inevitable'." Although I am still very young now, and there are many uncertain factors in my future development, one thing is certain. I want to take learning Chinese culture and studying Chinese knowledge as an important direction of my future efforts. I think this may be the "inevitability" of my fortune.

中国与我的职业生涯

［阿根廷］帕西奥
阿根廷教育部部长政治顾问，浙江大学硕士研究生

35 年前，我出生在阿根廷的瓜勒盖楚。

我是政治进程方向的政治学学士，毕业于阿根廷罗马天主教大学，我已经在这所大学任教 10 年了，是该校教政法、政治学和世界历史的副教

授。2016年我通过中国政府来华留学卓越奖学金项目，在浙江大学取得了中国研究专业的硕士学位。我的论文是《习近平与中国：对中国与拉美关系的影响和启示》，获得了“A”的评价。我还获得了拉丁美洲研究院公共政策硕士学位。目前，我是阿根廷迪特拉大学国际关系专业的博士研究生。

在我的职业生涯中，我在阿根廷和海外参与了多项社会调查，做了多场讲座。我发表论文多篇、学术著作多部，作品主题包括：拉美政治和经济，中国、美国和拉美的关系，体制分析和公共政策等。

近年来，我在公共和私营部门为高层提供政治分析和建议。2007年，我与一位大学同事共同创立了一所政治研究中心。同时，我是阿根廷国际关系委员会的成员和中国外交学院的客座教授。

2015年，我受中国驻阿根廷大使馆邀请，参加了由来自拉美国家的政治分析师和记者组成的代表团对中国进行了为期两周的访问。我们访问了北京、广州、深圳、昆明和云南省的一些城镇和乡村。我们拜访了地方政府官员和商人。

这是一次令人难忘的经历，改变了我的职业前景和研究兴趣。我了解了中国令人惊叹的文明和文化，这值得我钦佩和深入研究。中国的千年历史、中国文化的丰富和多样、中国人民不可思议的善良，都给我留下了深刻的印象。

造访中国之后，我意识到中国在过去的几十年里取得了巨大的发展，这对拉丁美洲的未来有着深刻的影响。中国和拉丁美洲经济互补，有很大的合作潜力。为了深化关系，增进了解，我相信拉美需要更多的中国学专家。幸运的是，中国一直在为促进双方的政治、文化和学术交流而努力。

在中国大使馆的推荐下，2016年，我有幸申请了中国政府来华留学卓越奖学金项目。几个月后，我飞往杭州留学一年，攻读浙江大学中国研究

专业的硕士学位。

我在浙江大学度过的那一年是我学术和人生的转折点。我从未在国外生活过，但幸运的是，我在中国一切顺利并获得了浙江大学中国研究硕士。

杭州是个独一无二的地方，它可能是中国最美丽的城市。我感到很幸运，能够在这里努力攻读硕士学位，同时享受生活。在杭州，我还学习了汉语。我特别喜欢中国书法课和中国当代史讲座。

尽管距离我的国家很远，但杭州对我而言就像是家一样。在杭州的这一年是我生命中难忘的日子，我将永远感谢这个机会。

启程回国前，我发现了自己获得了独特的职业优势。许多中国媒体和国际媒体开始联系我，我也收到了许多邀请，请我做一些关于中国和拉美关系方面的演讲。

前不久，我第三次来到了中国。我作为中国外交学院的客座教授，在北京待了一个月，在那里我向国际关系专业的本科生和博士生做了一系列讲座。

我非常荣幸能受邀参加 2018 青年汉学家研修计划。我希望它能让我更多地了解中国，结识来自世界各地的青年汉学家。我期待能为中国与拉美的合作做出进一步的贡献。

China and My Career

Patricio Giusto / Argentina

Ministry of Education, Argentina, Political advisor; Zhejiang University, Master

I was born in Gualeguaychú, Argentina, 35 years ago.

I am a Bachelor in Political Sciences specialized in Political Processes, graduated from the Pontifical Catholic University of Argentina, institution in which I have been an associate professor of Political Law, Political Science and World History for ten years.

In 2016, I completed a Master's degree in China Studies with the YES China Program scholarship, at Zhejiang University. My thesis, passed with "A" grade, was about: "Xi Jinping's political era in China: Implications and perspectives for the relation with Latin America".

I also have a Master's degree in Public Policies, from the Latin American Institute, among other postgraduate courses. Currently, I am a Ph.D candidate in International Studies at Di Tella University (Argentina).

Throughout my professional career, I have participated in several social investigations, as well as I have given many lectures, in Argentina and also abroad.

I am author of numerous academic paper and press publications, on topics such as: Latin-American politics and economy, the relations between China, the United States and Latin America, political systems analysis and public policies, among others.

In recent years, I have had the possibility to work both in the private and public sector, as a political analyst and advisor for top policy makers in my country.

In 2007, I co-founded my own center of political studies with a colleague from university. Besides, I am member of the Council on Foreign Relations of Argentina and visiting professor at China Foreign Affairs University (CFAU).

In 2015, I was invited by the Chinese Embassy in Argentina to join a delegation of political analysts and journalists from different Latin American countries, traveling to China for two exciting weeks.

We visited Beijing, Guangzhou, Shenzhen, Kunming and several smaller cities and rural areas in Yunnan province. We met local authorities, party officials and businessmen.

It was an unforgettable experience that changed my professional perspective and research interests. I discovered an amazing civilization and culture, which deserves to be admired and studied thoroughly.

I was deeply impressed by the millenary history, the immense richness and diversity of the Chinese culture and, mostly, the incredible kindness of the Chinese people.

After the 2015 trip, I realized the tremendous level of development achieved by China in the last decades and what it represents for the future of Latin America.

China and Latin America have a natural society, based on economic complementarities and with enormous potential for cooperation yet to be developed.

To continue expanding our relations and improve the mutual understanding, I am convinced that in Latin America we need more experts in China. Fortunately, China has been promoting more and more political, cultural and educational exchanges.

Thanks to that, with Chinese Embassy recommendation, in 2016 I had the opportunity to apply for the Youth of Excellence Scheme of China. A few months later, I was flying to Hangzhou to study for one-year period a Master of China Studies at Zhejiang University.

The year I spent at Zhejiang University was a turning point in my academic and personal life. I have never lived abroad before and, fortunately, everything went well and I graduated with a Master degree of Chinese Studies .

Hangzhou is a unique place in the world. Probably, it is the most beautiful city of China.

That's why I felt so lucky of being there and tried to take advantage of every day, while studying hard for the Master's degree.

I could also study a little Chinese language in Hangzhou. I especially enjoyed the Chinese calligraphy classes and the lectures about Chinese Contemporary History.

Despite being so far away from my country, during my stay in Hangzhou I felt all the time like If was at home. Those were unforgettable days of my life and I will be forever grateful for that opportunity.

Upon returning to my country, a prospect of professional growth was presented to me. I began to be required by the Chinese press and other international media, while I received numerous invitations to lecture on issues related to China and Latin America.

Recently, I traveled to China for the third time. I spent a month in Beijing as a visiting professor at China Foreign Affairs University, where I was able to present a series of lectures to undergraduate and Ph.D students of International Relations.

Finally, I am very happy now for this new invitation to participate in the Visiting Program for Young Sinologists 2018. I look forward of being part of this experience.

I hope it will give me the chance to learn more about China and meet young sinologists from other parts of the world. I expect to continue making my contributions to the cooperation between China and Latin America.

我与中国艺术

［爱尔兰］高雷蕾
布加勒斯特大学讲师

我在上大学的时候就开始对中国艺术感兴趣，我欣赏的艺术家有徐悲鸿、齐白石，还有蔡国强。之后，我遇见了一位新加坡朋友，她的名字是Faith。她向我展示了汉字“喜”字，双喜的喜，并解释了贴双喜的含义，那时候，我觉得汉字挺有意思，便走上了学习汉语的道路。

大学毕业之后，我一直从事艺术工作，工作之余我便在都柏林大学孔子学院学习汉语，我学会了一些简单的词，比如“你好”、“谢谢”，还有“火车站在哪儿”。

之后我就去了中国啦。第一次去中国，我学会了“饺子”“包子”和“好吃”这些词，都跟食物有关。

后来我和男朋友在香港待了三年。同样，在那儿，我还是从事艺术行业，同时也教英语。在香港，我认识了 Cindy。她说粤语，不过她在北京学过普通话，所以我们在一起做了语言交换，她教我汉语，我教她法语。

继香港之后，我去了伦敦，经营一家艺术画廊。其间，我发现一本台湾作家 Shaolan 的书，名叫“*Chineasy*”。意思是“Chinese”是“easy”的。通过这本书，我开始系统地学习汉字。

2015 年我回到爱尔兰，申请到了圣三一大学的汉语硕士课程，在学校，我认识了很多中国朋友，也交了一些学习中文的国际朋友。同时，我还修了教授的中国历史，以及田教授的汉语语言学课程。

研究生一共两年，其中有一学期，我去了北京大学交换学习。北京有好多美食，我吃到了“麻辣香锅”还有“煎饼果子。”

交换课程结束后，我便回到圣三一继续学习汉语。我的毕业论文描述的是 20 世纪 20 年代的漫画艺术，全称为“国统区上海政治漫画中的不平等现象”，主要研究对象是艺术家丰子恺以及杂志时代的漫画。论文提交后，我便去了威尔士一家学校做中国古董研究。

后来我的论文通过并被评为“优秀论文”。

现在我还继续从事艺术工作，并在都柏林大学学习中国绘画艺术。为庆祝 2018 年中国“狗年”新年，我的艺术工作室有很多以狗年为主题的活动。

到目前，我还没有去过中国的江南一带，听说那里非常美好，人文荟萃，是古代文人墨客常常称道的地方。真的很期待！

Chinese Art and I

Gray Heather / Ireland

Bucharest University, Lecturer

While studying art at university I became interested in Chinese artists such as Xu Beihong, Qi Baishi and Cai Guoqiang. Following this I met a girl from Singapore who showed me some Chinese characters, such as "double happiness". I loved the images and the story behind each character. After this I knew I had to learn more.

After finishing at university, I was working as an artist in Dublin. I also started a beginners Chinese evening course at the Confucius institute in University College Dublin (UCD). The following year, with only very basic Chinese, I decided to visit China for the first time. I travelled around for 2months with no real plan in mind. I picked up a few more important terms such as "jiaozi", "baozi", and "haochi".

After this, my boyfriend and I decided to live in Hong Kong. We lived there, on and off, for nearly 3 years.

In Hong Kong, I worked as an artist and as an English teacher. I did a language exchange with a woman named Cindy. She was Cantonese but had studied Mandarin in Beijing. I taught her conversational French and she taught me conversational Chinese.

After Hong Kong I moved to London to manage an art gallery. Here I found the book, *Chineasy*, by Shao Lan, a woman from Taiwan. Using this I really started to learn characters.

In 2015, I moved home to Ireland to study for a master's degree in Chinese studies. The M.Phil was 2 years in total and I met a host of amazing teachers and friends who taught me so much. I studied Chinese history under prof. Isabella Jackson and Chinese linguistics under prof. Adrian Tien. As part of the masters I spent one semester in Peking University studying Chinese. It was amazing and I learnt a huge amount, not least where to find the best mala xiang guo and jian bing in northeast Beijing.

I returned to Ireland after the exchange and wrote my dissertation on manhua in shanghai in the 1920's. It was called "Political Manhua: The Portrayal of Inequality in manhua (comics/cartoons) in Republican Era Shanghai". It focused on the artist, Feng Zikai, and the magazine *Shidai Manhua*.

After finishing my dissertation I attended a summer school in Wales which examined Chinese objects in small museum collections. In December I graduated with a distinction.

For the Chinese New Year this year, I put on a number of art workshops to welcome the year of the dog. They were part of the Dublin Chinese New Year Festival.

I am currently working as an artist again and studying Chinese painting at the Confucius institute in UCD.

I am very much looking forward to visiting Hangzhou and Jiangnan for the first time.

This is my Chinese story so far.

汉语塑造了我

［波兰］苏尔

格但斯克大学孔子学院汉语老师

2011 年十月初，在波兰一座叫波兹南的城市，秋天还未走远。三号那一天，一个二十岁的红发姑娘、单纯的理想主义者坐着电车朝学校走去。一会儿她就要成为汉学专业的本科生了，她根本不会想到，那一天会改变

她的一生。

这个小姑娘就是七年前的我。我的中国故事就是我和汉语的故事。

至于我和汉语的关系，可以说那不是一见钟情，而是经过一个缓慢的过程而产生出来的成熟感情，每当我想分析那种感情，就能联想到我父母谈恋爱的时候。他们俩性格完全不同，高中时妈妈是个乖学霸，爸爸是个淘气鬼——他们一直都讨厌彼此，直到老师派妈妈帮助爸爸准备高考，他们渐渐相互熟识，彼此产生了一种温柔的好奇心，但是对爱大彻大悟却需要很多年，最后这种感觉变成了一个美好的爱情故事——我和中文也是同样的情形：汉语具有好听的声调，我又不会唱歌；汉语中注重的是地位，我还只是个普通的博士生；汉语有补语，那我呢，对“捕鱼”不太感兴趣——您说，汉语与我不是正相反吗？不过，连物理学理论也证明：对立的物体相互吸引——我还是相信科学吧。

突然间，我与汉语终于开始配合默契了。

我在学汉语的第三年才取得了突破性的进展——那年是我第一次来中国，是我亲身体验到中国文化的一年，是我认识我后来的导师的一年，是对汉语的爱突然涌上我心头的一年。在山东烟台鲁东大学国际教育学院院长胡晓清教授的支持与指导下，我变成了汉教专业的硕士研究生。

可以说，我在中国学习和生活的难忘场面就是汉办组织的汉教英雄会。导师早就知道我是个好强的人，也一直相信我这个丫头的能力，就派我参加首届比赛。第一阶段比赛结束后，我仍然不敢相信，自己能从 700 名选手中脱颖而出，进入前 140 名，更不要说能从 140 名选手中胜出，进入 50 强。来自五湖四海的汉教同学们的汉语能力远远超出了我的想象，我感觉快要被他们的天才碾压了。

六月的北京让我感到又热又累，头昏脑涨，心几乎提到了嗓子眼。那颗心中只想着一件事儿，那就是："老师们为我付出了这么多的努力，不要让他们失望"。过了几轮比赛，有欢笑、有泪水，我又发烧，又激动，在如此巨大的压力下，我又从 50 强进入 32 强。那时候我感觉太不可思议了，没能控制住自己的感情，泪如雨下。我也不知道是因为高兴还是因为害怕！不过，我还是决定继续展现最好的自己，继续坚持，奋斗到底。

准备下一轮比赛时，我又从导师、朋友和队员们那里得到了强有力的支持，令人感动的是，其实没有什么"对手"，选手们早就成了我的朋友，我们成了汉语国际教育大家庭的亲人。在这样亲切的气氛下，我不知不觉地出现在了 16 强榜单中，这也就是全国外研 8 强、中外 16 强阶段，也是我在这个比赛当中的最后一个阶段。被淘汰后，在十天里只睡了十二个小时觉的我终于松了一口气，能从另一个角度来看所做的一切，也终于开始相信自己的能力了。

那场比赛对我具有里程碑的意义。它让我开阔了眼界，我除了学到有关中国文化和汉语的很多知识，更重要的是通过这场比赛发现了真实的自己，从此我什么都不怕了。现在，当面对生活中的困难时，我就会想起那年六月的北京，那场百舸争流的比赛，然后对自己说：这件事儿你都做得到，还怕什么呢？这次经验让我真正地体验到了中国和汉语的力量，它塑造了我的价值观，也塑造了我。

2018 年九月，在中国一座叫杭州的城市，一个红发姑娘、汉语教师、中波翻译、在读博的青年汉学家正在发言，怀念着七年前的自己。她还保留着那份初心，而且终于有了去追求自己中国梦的勇气。她知道，她与中国的故事才刚刚开始，一切未完待续。

Chinese Language Shapes Me

Sroka-Gradziel Anna Maria / Poland

Confucius Institute, Gdansk University, Chinese Teacher

In early October 2011, in a Polish city called Poznan, autumn was not far away. On the 3rd, a 20-year-old girl with red hair, a simple idealist, went towards the school by tram. Soon she will become an undergraduate majoring in Sinology. She never thought that that day would change her life.

This little girl was me. My story of China is the story of me and Chinese language.

As for my relationship with Chinese, it can be said that it is not love at first sight, but a mature feeling produced through a gradual process. Whenever I want to analyze that feeling, I can associate it with my parents' love. They have totally different personalities. When they were in high school, my mother was a bully and my father was a naughty guy — they always hated each other. Until the teacher sent my mother to help him prepare for the college entrance examination, they gradually got to know each other and developed a kind of gentle curiosity towards each other. But it took many years for them to have a thorough understanding of love. Finally, this feeling turned into a beautiful love story — my relationship with Chinese just the same: Chinese has a pleasant tone, but I can't sing; Chinese focuses on status, but I'm just an ordinary doctoral student; Chinese has complements, but I'm not very interested in "fishing" — "Bu Yu" pronounced in Chinese — don't you think Chinese is opposite to me? But even the theory of physics proves that opposites attract each other — I believe in science.

All of a sudden, Chinese and I finally began to cooperate.

I made a breakthrough in my third year of learning Chinese. That year was my first visit to China, a year when I experienced Chinese culture, a year when I met my later tutor, and a year when my love for Chinese suddenly surged into my heart. Under the support and guidance of Professor Hu Xiaoqing, Dean of School of international education, Ludong University, I became a Master of Chinese education.

It can be said that the climax of my study and life in China was to take part in the contest organized by Hanban. My tutor knew that I was a strong person for a long time, and always believed in my ability, so he sent me to participate in the first competition. After the first stage, I still can't believe that I can stand out from 700 players and enter the top 140, let alone win from 140 players and enter the top 50. In the competition, I realized that the Chinese ability of the students from all over the world is far beyond my imagination, and I feel that I am about to be crushed by their talents.

I felt hot and tired, dizzy in June in Beijing, and my heart almost reached my throat. That heart only think of one thing, that is: "the teachers have paid so much effort for me, don't let them down.". After several rounds of competition, there were laughter and tears. I had a fever and excitement. Under such great pressure, I entered the top 32 from the top 50 of Chinese and foreign research institutes. At that time, I felt too incredible, unable to control their feelings, tears. I don't know whether it's because I'm happy or because I'm afraid! However, I still decided to continue to show my best self in the aspect of Han education, continue to persist and strive to the end.

When preparing for the next round of competition, I got strong support from my tutors, friends and team members. What is moving is that there are no "rivals" there. The players have long been my friends and relatives of the big family of Chinese international education. In such a cordial atmosphere, I unconsciously appeared in the list of the top 16, which is also the stage of the top 8 of foreign research and the top 16 of China and foreign countries, and the last stage of this competition. After being eliminated, after sleeping for only 12 hours in 10 days, I finally felt relieved that I could see what I had done from another angle, and I finally began to believe in my ability.

That game was a milestone for me. It broadened my horizons. In addition to learning a lot about Chinese culture and Chinese, what's more, I found my true self through this competition. From then on, I'm not afraid of anything. Now, when facing the difficulties in life, I will think of the competition in Beijing in June that year, and then say to myself: you can do it all, what are you afraid of? This experience let me really experience the power of China and Chinese, it shaped my values, shaped me.

In September 2018, in a Chinese city called Hangzhou, a young Sinologist with red hair, a Chinese teacher, a Sino Polish translator, and a doctoral degree was speaking, remembering herself seven years ago. She still retains her original intention and finally has the courage to pursue her Chinese dream. She knows that although you have heard the end of her speech, her story with China has just begun, and it is still to be continued.

学习中文改变了我的生活

［俄罗斯］爱琳

俄罗斯高等经济学院研究生

我小时候住在俄罗斯远东，这个地区离中国的黑龙江省很近。我们镇上有很多中国人，还有中国货、中国餐馆等。小的时候的很多东西都记不清了，但是中国人的微笑和他们的友好是我从那时起就无法忘记的记忆。

2002年，我和父母从远东搬走，在我们离开之前，我和爸爸沿着阿穆尔河堤散步。河的一边是俄罗斯领土，另

一边是中国领土。我们站在俄罗斯的土地上，看着对面中国的城市，我父亲告诉我："十年前，我和你妈妈来到这里。河对岸几乎什么也没有。现在你可以看到这些发展中的城市。才十年！你能想象吗？这是奇迹吗？"我印象深刻。

几年后，我上学了并有了新朋友，而我的父母去了中国。中国让他们印象深刻，所以，他们决定带我和妹妹一起去中国。于是，2006 年冬天，我第一次来到中国，中国给我留下了不可磨灭的印象。对我这个来自乌拉尔南部一个小城市的女孩来说，这是一件令人惊奇和难以置信的事情。我的同学从未见过中国人，对他们来说，中国是一个陌生的国家。他们都对我关于中国的故事很感兴趣。当我给他们讲这个国家的时候，我试着说我自己的"汉语"。那时我还不会说中文，但朋友们说我的"中文"听起来像真的（没关系，他们从来没听过）。我们在笑，但同时，我相信有一天我会学会的。

我毕业后进入圣彼得堡州立大学学习公共关系。第二年，我决定去孔子学院学习中文，即使是对我来说这也是个很大挑战，我的朋友和同学中没有人学习中文。但我问自己：“为什么不呢？”我应该去尝试。

现在看来，这是我最正确的决定之一。由于学习中文，我的生活发生了变化。我对世界、文化、社会和政治结构、国际交流、全球经济发展有了更多的了解。我去了很多新地方，认识了新朋友。我在中国学习了一年，不仅发现了这个神奇的国家的很多新事物，也发现了我自己的新兴趣。

我现在的研究领域是东方研究。我专注于跨文化交流、中国市场以及中国年轻人的消费行为。

Learning Chinese Changed My Life

Adelina Ishmuratova / Russia
Russia Higher School of Economics, Graduate Student

When I was a child I lived in Russia's Far East, this region is very close to Heilongjiang province in China. There were a lot of Chinese people, Chinese goods, food and so on in our town. As I was small, I do not remember a lot, but the smiles of Chinese people and their friendliness are the memories I cannot forget since that time.

In 2002, my parents and I moved from Far East. Before we left, my dad and me had walked along Amur River embankment. It is Russian territory on the one side of the river, and another side is Chinese land. We were standing on the Russian ground and we were looking at Chinese city, and my father told me: "Ten years ago your mom and I came here. There was almost nothing on the opposite side of the river. Now you can see the developing city. Just ten years! Can you imagine? Is it a miracle?" I was very impressed.

Some years left, I went to school, I had new friends and my parents visited China. They were so impressed, so, they decided to bring my sister and me to visit China too. Thus, in winter 2006, I came to China for the first time and China made an indelible impression on me. For the girl from a small city in the South of Ural it was something amazing and unbelievable. My classmates had never met Chinese people and for them China was the unknown country. All of them were very interested in my stories about China. When I was telling them about the country I tried to speak my own "Chinese language". That time I could not speak Chinese, but friends told my "Chinese" sounded like real (does not matter they have never heard it). We were laughing but in the same time, I was confident that one day I would learn it.

I finished the school and I entered to St. Petersburg State University to study public relation. On the second year I decided to take the course in Confucius Institute. It was absolutely unexpected even for me, no one from my friends or classmates study Chinese. But I asked myself: "Why not?" and I tried.

Now I can say that it was one of the best decisions. Due to learning Chinese my life has changed. I learnt more about the world, new culture, social and political structure, communication, economic development. I visited new places and met new people. I spent year in China and I discovered new things not only about this amazing country but about myself, too.

In current period of time I am doing my master in the field of oriental studies. And I focus on cross-cultural communication, marketing in China, consumer behavior of young Chinese.

在中国求学，在罗马尼亚教汉语

［罗马尼亚］木固烈
布加勒斯特大学讲师

我与中国的故事是从巧克力和电影开始的，如今已有30多年了。20世纪80年代，罗马尼亚进口商品少得很，有时买得到从中国进口的巧克力或牙膏。我已不记得巧克力的味道，牙膏更不用说，但还记得包装上的

汉字看上去特别神奇，让十来岁的我赞叹不已。电影院偶尔播放中国武打片，像《武当》或《侠女十三妹》，名字我还记得清清楚楚，看了好几遍，不是因为演员打得很厉害，而是他们说的那种语言实在太好听了！在我儿时就意识到世界上真的有中国这个国家，并决定一定要去那里看看。

随着时光流逝，儿时的好奇心成为我今天的职业。我上了布加勒斯特大学中文系之后，获得了赴华留学奖学金，本科、硕士学位都是从北京语言大学获得的。一直到今天，我不是去北京，而是回北京，就像回家一样，虽然今天的北京跟20年前的完全不同。

大学毕业之后，我离开了中国，但我与中国的故事还没结束，我也不再是故事中的人物，而是故事的叙述者。我在罗马尼亚国内拿到了博士学位后从事汉语教育工作，一开始教汉语语法和口语，后来教中国历史文化、现当代文学、中国翻译史和汉语语言学。学生一年比一年多，一届比一届难对付。原来我们布大中文系是我的国家唯一教汉语的地方，现在共有四所国立大学和一所民办大学都开设了汉语专业，此外在罗马尼亚还有四个孔子学院。

我认为我的责任不仅仅是教学生汉语和中国文化，更是激发和提高他们对中国的兴趣。他们进入大学的时候，关于中国的事情知道得比我当时多得多，他们与中国的故事不再是从吃巧克力、看武打片开始的，而是去中国餐厅、上网或买中国制造的东西开始。汉语虽然学起来不容易，但是很值得，这是我每年、每次有新的学生跟新的要求都要考虑的一个问题。

这是我与中国的故事的一个叙事线索。近几年，我的国家的出版社对中国当代文学非常感兴趣，增加了我和我的同事翻译文学的机会。现在不仅看或教余华、莫言、苏童、徐则臣等著名作家的作品，我还有幸认识了他们，跟他们聊过天、喝过茶。我给大三的学生上文学课的时候，经常告诉他们，这个作家人怎么样怎么样，你们一定要好好儿地看他的书。

最后我想跟大家分享我认为是让我最高兴的一句恭维话。说这句话的中国朋友根本没有恭维我的意思，不过呢……有一次回北京，跟朋友吃饭侃大山，有人突然跟我说“妈呀，你真像北京人一样，贫！”我很高兴，看起来我中国化了。

Studying in China and Teaching Chinese in Romania

Mugur Zotea / Romania

Bucharest University, Lecturer

My story with China started with chocolate and movies, and now it has been more than 30 years. In the 1980s, Romania imported very few goods. Sometimes it could buy chocolate or toothpaste imported from China. I can't remember the taste of chocolate, not to mention toothpaste, but I can still remember that the Chinese characters on the package looked so magical that I was in my 10's. Chinese martial arts movies are occasionally shown in cinemas, such as Wudang or thirteen chivalrous girls. I can still remember their names clearly. I have watched them several times, not because the actors fight very hard, but because the language they speak is so beautiful! When I was a child, I realized that there was China in the world and decided to go there.

As time goes by, childhood curiosity becomes my today's profession. After entering the Chinese Department of Bucharest University, I won a scholarship to study in China. Both my bachelor's and master's degrees were obtained from Beijing Language and Culture University. Now, I am not going to Beijing, but going back to Beijing, just like going home, although today's Beijing is totally different from 20 years ago.

After graduated from University, I left China, but my story with China is not over, and I am no longer the character in the story, but the narrator of the story. After I got my doctor's degree in Romania, I began to teach Chinese grammar and oral English. Later, I taught Chinese history and culture, modern and contemporary literature, Chinese translation history and Chinese linguistics. Students are getting more and more year by year, and each year is more and more difficult to deal with. Originally, the Chinese Department of Bubu University was the only place to teach Chinese in our country. Now, there are four national universities and one private university with Chinese major. In addition, there are four Confucius Institutes in Romania.

I think my responsibility is not only to teach students Chinese and Chinese culture, but also to stimulate and improve their interest in China. When they entered the University, they knew much more about China than I did at that time. Their story with China no longer started from eating chocolate and watching martial arts movies, but from going to Chinese restaurants, surfing the Internet or buying things made in China. Although learning Chinese is not easy, it is worth it. This is a problem that I have to consider every year and every time I have new students and new requirements.

This is a narrative clue of my story with China. In recent years, the publishing houses in my country are very interested in Chinese contemporary literature, which has increased the opportunities for me and my colleagues to translate literature. Now I have not only read or taught the works of Yu Hua, Mo Yan, Su Tong, Xu Zechen and other famous writers, but also met them, chatted with them and had tea. When I give literature lessons to junior students, I often tell them how the writer is. You must read his books carefully.

Before I finish, I would like to share with you what I think is my most happy compliment. The Chinese friends who said this didn't mean to compliment me at all, but Once I went back to Beijing and had dinner with my friends, someone suddenly said to me, "Oh my god, you are so wordy like a Beijinger!" I'm happy. It makes me even more look like Chinese.

我与中国文学、历史

[越南] 吴越环

越南社会科学院文学研究所研究员

2013年9月我来到成都，在四川大学开始求学的旅程，当时我24岁。也就是说，我人生中最好的年华、最具生命力的时光是在中国度过的。大家都知道，24岁至30岁是一个男孩慢慢成熟、慢慢成长为一个男人的重要阶段。在《论语·为政》篇中，孔子云："吾十有五，而志于学。三十而立。四十而不惑。五十而知天命。六十而耳顺。七十而从心所欲，不逾矩。"24岁时的我刚刚完成硕士研究生的学业，对于人生之路，我充满了自信、充满了希望，同时也充满了各种坎坷、困惑与迷茫。2013年暑假，我做出了自己人生中具有标杆性的决定，那就是暂停在越南社会科学院文学所的工作，来到百年名校四川大学攻读博士学位。由于不是外国语专业出身，我必须学习一年的汉语预科，而我的汉学研究之路可以说就是从那一年开启的。四川大学海外教育学院教师胡翼老师是我在中国留学期间的第一位汉语老师，在他尽责热情的教导之下，对汉语完全陌生的我学会了用汉语进行简单的沟通与交流。到了博士二年级的时候，我几乎已修完了高级汉语的所有课程。

2014年9月，我正式进入博士阶段学习，成为中国著名学者曹顺庆教授的第一名越南籍博士研究生。在先生的培养之下，我慢慢走上了比较文学与世界文学的学术道路，立志成为一名汉学研究者。在曹顺庆、赵毅衡、徐新建、王晓路、闫家等一批中国著名学者的课堂上，我不仅有机会系统化地研读十三经、《文心雕龙》、中国古典文论等东方经典知识，还学到了文学人类学、文学符号学等西方现代学科。

还记得第一次和导师见面的时候，我心情十分复杂。能成为曹顺庆先生的弟子肯定是我的幸运，在先生的指导下，我肯定会学到很多的东西。但在自豪和骄傲的同时，我也非常担心，我要怎么才能被老师认可，我该怎么才能最快地融入曹门这个雄厚而强大的队伍之中。这些问题让我几天都吃不好、睡不着。后来我决定尽可能努力，反正我也管不了那么多了。在和导师见面的那一天，所有的担忧和焦虑很快消失了。跟我想象的不一样，我的导师不是一个高冷、难以接触的人，反而非常大方、温和与亲切。我心里的那块石头不知不觉地落了下来。博士一年级时的主要任务是把博士培养方案所规定的21学分都修完。就在这一学年，我非常荣幸能参加曹顺庆教授亲自授课的平台课“中华文化原典读本：十三经注疏”。这门课程每周只上两大节课，但比每天都要上的其他课程压力还大。我刚来到中国，连很多简体字都不认识，怎么能读懂原典呢，而且还是上海古籍出版社出版的宋代版本。但在这段艰难的学习过程中，我收到了同门师兄弟姐妹无私的鼓励和帮助。是他们的热情和耐心帮我度过那一难关。现在想起那门课，心里那种恍惚的滋味还依旧难受。

在四川大学读书的那些年，我走遍了学校的三个校区。望江校区的北大门、荷花池，华西校区的钟楼、图书馆，还有江安校区的长桥和明远湖等地，都从陌生逐渐地变成了熟悉。但我慢慢融入这块土地之时，也就是我们将要说再见的时刻。有人说人生不过是一场梦，如果真是这样，那么我在成都、在川大度过的这四年时间，便是我这一生最美妙的一场梦。

我从小就喜欢读书，文学、历史及哲学等相关书籍都是我最为喜欢的。同年的朋友一直沉迷在日本漫画的世界，我则被历史传说及小说中的各种离奇奥妙的情节吸引，而无法自拔。高三时，有人送我一本《东方文明史》，从这本书中，我知晓人类之史从何而起，同时也知道世界各国文明如何萌生、兴盛和衰亡。而世界上最早出现的四大文明之中，只有黄河流域文明，也就是中华文明，能够拥有五千年连续不断的历史传承。这个国家和我的祖国越南还有着几千年友好的邦交。于是，在不知不觉中，我开始寻找并阅读了大量跟中国历史、文学、文化等有关的图书。秦始皇、司马迁、项羽、刘邦、刘备、曹操、孙权、朱元璋、孙中山、毛泽东、邓小平等中国历史上著名人物均为我所熟悉。孔子的“三纲五常”、老子的“道德经”，以及中国佛教历史人物的六祖禅宗慧能法师，都是我非常喜欢探索和研究的对象。可以说，越南文学，特别是越南民间文学，养育了我，让我健康、善良地长大，中国思想文化和文学则让我懂得更多人生哲理，丰富了我的心灵，也让我在汉学研究道路上能走得更远、飞得更高。

我记得在2017届本科及研究生毕业典礼上，当时四川大学校长谢和平院士曾嘱咐我们：“厚道比聪明更重要”，“四川大学研究生应该成为经世之才”。两句寄语，德才兼备，以德为先，那也就是中华民族伟大传统文化的核心价值观，更是对人类负起担当和责任的一种理念。“海纳百川、有容乃大”，在中华文化博大精深的知识海洋里，我变得更加渺小，但同时也有了一名知识分子应有的修养和气质。

在中国留学的那些年，寒暑假期我都争取出去走走。我去过拥有五千年历史的古都西安、游过千年历史的文化名城北京，也看过百年历史文化的大都市上海。我还有机会到杭州体验宋朝文化，游西湖十景，到重庆游览长江、赏山城的夜景，到桂林欢游于山水，到南京拜谒中山陵、欣赏中国六朝古都之美景。不管走到哪里，我看到的不仅是壮观的山水、巍峨的楼阁，更是中国人的热情与微笑。我的独行之游也就因此而变得更加有趣。

时间煮雨，我与中国的相遇如今已 5 年有余，如同 2013 年刚来到中国时的愿望，我仍努力在汉学研究领域的田野上耕耘除草。前方之路任重道远，而我的中国故事还会继续下去。

Chinese Literature, History and I

Ngo Viet Hoan / Vietnam

Institute of Literature, Vietnamese Academy of Social Sciences, Researcher

I came to Chengdu in September 2013 and started my study in China at Sichuan University when I was 24 years old. As we all know, the 20s to 30s period is an important stage for a boy to grow up and become a man. In other words, the best years and the most vital time of my life were spent in China. In the *Analects of Confucius* · *Weizheng*, it says, "I was 15 years old, but I was determined to learn. a man should be independent at the age of thirty. at forty, I had no doubts. at fifty, I knew the decrees of heaven. at sixty, my ear was an obedient organ for the reception of truth. at seventy, I could follow what my heart desired, without transgressing what was right." When I was 24 years old, I had just finished my master's degree. I was full of confidence, hope, frustration, confusion and confusion. In the summer vacation of 2013, I made a benchmarking decision in my life, that is, to suspend my work in the Literature Institute of the Vietnamese Academy of Social Sciences and go to Sichuan University to study for a doctorate. Because I was not a foreign language major, I had to study Chinese for one year, and I started my Sinology research in that year. Hu Yi, a teacher of the school of overseas education of Sichuan University, was the first Chinese teacher when I was studying in China. Under his responsible and enthusiastic teaching, I was completely unfamiliar with Chinese and learned to use Chinese for simple communication. By the second year of my Ph.D., I had almost finished all the advanced Chinese courses.

In September 2014, I officially entered the doctoral stage and became the first Vietnamese doctoral student of Professor Cao Shunqing, a famous Chinese scholar. Under the cultivation of my husband, I gradually embarked on the academic road of comparative literature and world literature, determined to become a Sinologist. In the classroom of Cao Shunqing, Zhao Yiheng, Xu Xinjian, Wang Xiaolu, Yan Jia and other famous Chinese scholars, I not only had the opportunity to systematically study the thirteen classics, Wenxindiaolong, Chinese classical literary theory and other oriental classical knowledge, but also learned modern western disciplines such as literary anthropology and literary semiotics.

I still remember when I met my tutor the first time, I was very nervous. It must be my luck to be Mr. Cao Shunqing's student. Under his guidance, I certainly learn a lot. But at the same time, I am also very worried about how I can be recognized by teachers and how I can integrate into the strong and powerful team of Cao as soon as possible. These problems made me unable to eat and sleep well for several days. Later, I decided to try my best. Anyway, I couldn't manage that much. But on the day of meeting with the tutor, all the worries and anxieties quickly disappeared. Unlike what I imagined, my tutor is not a cold, hard to reach person, but very generous, gentle and kind. The stone in my heart fell down unconsciously. The main task of the first year doctor is to complete the 21 credits required by the doctoral training program. In this academic year, I am very honored to participate in the platform course "Chinese culture original Classics: Notes on the thirteen classics" taught by Professor Cao Shunqing. This course has only two major classes a week, but it's more stressful than any other course you have to take every day. I just came to China, and I don't know many simplified Chinese characters. How can I understand the original book? It's also the Song Dynasty version published by Shanghai ancient books publishing house. But in this difficult time, I received the encouragement and help from my brothers and sisters. It was their enthusiasm and patience that helped me through that. Now I think of that course, the feeling of trance in my heart is still uncomfortable.

In those years of studying in Sichuan University, I went all over the three campuses of the University. The north gate and lotus pond of Wangjiang campus, the bell tower and Library of West China campus, the Changqiao and Mingyuan lake of Jiang'an campus have gradually changed from strangeness to familiarity. But when I slowly integrate into this land, that is the moment when we are going to say goodbye. Some people say that life is just a dream. If that is true, then the four years I spent in Chengdu and Sichuan University are the most wonderful dream of my life.

I like reading books since I was a child. Literature, history and philosophy are my favorite books. In the same year, my friends had been addicted to the world of Japanese comics, while I was attracted by various strange and mysterious plots in historical legends and novels. In the third year of senior high school, someone sent me a history of Oriental civilization. From this history of civilization, I knew where the history of human beings came from, and how civilizations around the world sprouted, flourished and declined. Among the five earliest civilizations in the world, only the Yellow River Valley civilization, that is, the Chinese civilization, can have 5000 years of continuous historical inheritance. This country and my country Vietnam still have friendly diplomatic relations for thousands of years. So, unconsciously, I began to look for and read a lot of books related to Chinese history, literature, culture and so on. I am familiar with such famous historical figures as Qin Shihuang, Sima Qian, Xiang Yu, Liu Bang, Liu Bei, Cao Cao, Sun Quan, Zhu Yuanzhang, Sun Yat Sen, Mao Zedong and Deng Xiaoping. Confucius's "three cardinal guides and five constant principles", Laozi's "Dao Te Ching", and master Huineng, the sixth patriarch of Zen Buddhism, who is a historical figure of Chinese Buddhism, are the objects I like to explore and study very much. It can be said that Vietnamese literature, especially Vietnamese folk literature, has nurtured me and made me grow up healthily and kindly, while Chinese ideology, culture and literature have made me understand more life philosophy, enriched my soul, and enabled me to go further and fly higher on the road of Sinology research.

I remember that at the 2017 graduation ceremony for undergraduates and postgraduates, academician Xie Heping, President of Sichuan University, once told us: "kindness is more important than intelligence" and "Postgraduates of

Sichuan university should become statesmen". In two words, the core values of the great traditional culture of the Chinese nation are the combination of ability and political integrity and the priority of morality, which is also a concept of taking responsibility and responsibility for human beings. In the vast ocean of knowledge of Chinese culture, I have become even smaller, but at the same time, I have the cultivation and temperament that an intellectual should have.

In those years when I studied in China, I tried to go out for a walk during summer and winter holidays. Now I have been to Xi'an, an ancient capital with 5000 years of history, Beijing with 1000 years of history and culture, and Shanghai with 100 years of history and culture. I also have the opportunity to experience the culture of Song Dynasty in Hangzhou, to visit ten sceneries of West Lake, to visit the Yangtze River in Chongqing, to enjoy the night scenery of mountain city, to enjoy the scenery in Guilin, to visit Dr. Sun Yat-sen Mausoleum in Nanjing, and to enjoy the beautiful scenery of the ancient capital of Six Dynasties in China. No matter where I go, what I see is not only the spectacular landscapes and towering pavilions, but also the enthusiasm and smile of the Chinese people. So my solo tour became more interesting.

It has been more than five years since I met China. Just like my wish when I first came to China in 2013, I still work hard in the field of Sinology. There is a long way to go, and my Chinese story will continue.

我与中国的特殊情缘

［塔吉克斯坦］阿斯列金

塔吉克斯坦国立大学班主任

我与中国有着一份特殊的情缘，回忆起这段经历，我有时会问自己，我是不是在梦中。

2003 年我作为塔吉克斯坦国防部外事局的一名中尉被派往解放军外国

语学院学习汉语。当时我们的国防部外事局已经有一名军官在中国学习过一年的汉语，他给我们介绍，中国是一个友好、美丽的国家。但是大家对中国的了解是少之又少，在大家的印象中只有电影里见到的李小龙、李连杰、成龙。在这位前辈的推荐下，我来到了美丽的古都洛阳，来到了花园式的洛阳外国语学院。我的中国情缘就从这里开始了。

由于 9 月 9 日是塔吉克斯坦的国庆节，我们承担祖国国庆的任务，所以到洛阳时已是 10 月初，落下的功课学校专门安排老师在国庆假期间为我们补课。给我们补课的是一位年轻的中国老师，我们一直以为她是大学生。在这位老师耐心的帮助下，我们很快就赶上了大家的进度。

正式开始上课了，第一节是初级汉语听力。没想到走进教室的正是给我们补课的那位“大学生”。后来大家也许能猜到……我爱上了这位“大学生”。说到我们能走到一起也是一波三折，由于国籍、民族、信仰等多方面的差异，她的父母也就是我的岳父母非常反对，那时我的汉语水平还非常有限，我去拜访了岳父母，还经常给他们打电话，最终得到了他们的同意。我们领了结婚证，那也是一段难忘的记忆。在一次去北京的参观旅行途中，我与一位同学找到了塔吉克驻中国大使馆的朋友，了解如何在使馆领取结婚证，然后让国内的朋友给我准备相关材料。2005 年 5 月 9 日正好是塔吉克斯坦的宪法日，我们在塔吉克斯坦驻中国大使馆领取了结婚证，大使亲自为我们颁发了编号为 01 的结婚证并祝福我们。大使说这是他颁发的第一例中塔婚姻的结婚证。那时我们从来没考虑过组建家庭的种种困难，就是在爱情力量的指引下一直往前。作为学生的我当时没有经济能力给妻子一个美丽的婚礼，这是我觉得特别亏欠她和岳父母的一点。2005 年 7 月我回到塔吉克斯坦，8 月妻子来到了杜尚别，在这里的两所大学任教。我们两人白手起家，从一无所有走到现在，妻子来到塔吉克自学了塔吉克语，后来由于工作中表现突出，先调到新疆师范大学工作后又通过了孔子学院的考试成了孔子学院的一名公派教师。如今我也跟随她进入了塔吉克斯坦民族大学，成为一名汉语教师。中国有句古话“百年修得同船渡，千年修得共枕眠”。时常早上醒来，我在想，这是梦吗？我娶了中国妻子。说到我们的幸福生活，我想最重要的是中塔两国有着悠久的历史文化，两国在文化价值观方面有着很大的认同，从领导层到民众都有着深厚的友谊。当时给我们颁发结婚证的大使说，据史书记载在 3500 年前曾有一位中国公主嫁到塔吉克斯坦。

2005 年时我们的工资特别低，大概是 20 美元，根本买不起房，也租不起房，当时的国防部长了解到这样的情况后特批给我每月 100 美元的住房补助，他说“中国给了我们这么多的援助，不能让中国媳妇在塔吉克受委屈”。他与其他军队领导多次出访和接待中国客人时都把我带在身边，并自豪地给中方客人介绍我这个中国女婿。塔吉克的家庭都是大家庭，一般父母都有 7、8 个孩子，大家都住在一起。部长曾不止一次地提醒我，中国的社会现状与我们不同，对妻子一定要耐心地解释，不要让大家庭的生活方式给她带来困惑。2006 年我回到中国继续进修，在进修期间，妻子住院、我父亲去世，是同事和领导守在手术室外等待……往事历历在目，每次我们聊起这些日子，我和妻子都非常感动，感动于我们两国有着如此好的关系，所以我们的婚姻才会如此幸福。2010—2012 年我负责中国国防部援建塔吉克国防部“军官之家”大楼建设的塔方对接翻译工作，在“军官之家”的援建石碑上有着一段塔文，我将它翻译为“种下友谊之树，结出丰硕果实”。

塔吉克斯坦的许多民生工程都是中资企业投资或者中国政府援建的。塔吉克之前面临着严重的电力资源缺口，冬季都要限时供电，自新疆特变电工热电厂建成后，给塔吉克斯坦的千家万户送来了光明与温暖，冬季不再停电了，而且有了水暖。塔吉克斯坦的路况不太好，中国路桥、北新路桥给塔吉克修了多段重要的交通线路，82 小区的高架桥也将很快竣工通车了。妻子说“这几年塔吉克斯坦有了天翻地覆的变化”，我跟她开玩笑说“这些都来自我的亲家啊”。塔吉克民众对中国人民勤劳吃苦的精神赞誉有加，中国产品遍布塔吉克市场，“中国制造”大大降低了我们的生活成本，提高了我们的生活质量，中国公司的投资入驻提高了我国的就业率，为塔吉克民众提供了更多的工作机会，很多人都以到中资企业工作为荣。汉语热就更不用说，越来越多的家庭选择把自己的孩子送到孔子学院学习，能到中国留学成为越来越多的年轻人的梦想，汉语正在给我们的生活带来日新月异的变化。

A Special Love Relationship in China

Normakhmadov Asliddin / Tajikistan

Tajik National University, Class Adviser

I have experienced a love relationship in China that sometimes I thought it was a dream when recalling.

In 2003, as a lieutenant in the Foreign Affairs Bureau of the Ministry of Defense of Tajikistan, I was sent to the Foreign Languages Institute of the People's Liberation Army to learn Chinese. At that time, an officer who had ever studied Chinese in China for one year told us that China was a friendly and beautiful country. But we knew little about China, and we only knew it from the movie characters like Bruce Lee, Jet Li and Jackie Chan. Listening to his recommendation, I came to the beautiful ancient capital Luoyang and came to the garden-like Luoyang Institute of Foreign Languages, where my Chinese journey started.

Since September 9th is the National Day of Tajikistan, we have been tasked to celebrate the National Day. Thus, we didn't arrived at Luoyang until early October. The school arranged a teacher to make up for the missed lessons during the National holiday for us. Our remedial teacher was a young Chinese teacher, and so young that we took it for granted that she's a college student. With her help, we caught up with others soon.

The first Class began with the elementary Chinese listening. To our surprise, the teacher for this class was that "college student" who gave the make-up classes for us. Later on, as you can probably guess...I fell in love with her. Due to the differences in nationality, ethnic, religion and other aspects, her parents, namely my parents-in-law, were strongly opposed to our relationship. At that time, my Chinese was still very limited. I went to my parents-in-law's home, made phone calls to them, and finally got their consent. Looking back to the experience in getting a marriage certificate, it was really memorable. It was on a trip to Beijing, one of my classmates and I found a friend worked at the Tajik Embassy in China. We learned how to get a marriage certificate in the embassy, and then asked my domestic friends to prepare relevant materials for me. On May 9th, which was the Constitution Day of Tajikistan, we received our marriage certificate at the Embassy of Tajikistan in China. The ambassador personally issued the marriage certificate numbered 01 to us and blessed us. The ambassador said it was the first China Tajikistan marriage certificate he had issued. At that time, we have not taken all the difficulties of forming a family into consideration, but went ahead with love. As a student, I did not have enough money to give my wife a grand wedding, which I felt particularly indebted to her and my parents-in-law. On July, 2005, I came back to Tajikistan, and then my wife moved to Dushanbe the next month, where she taught at two universities. Both of us were started from scratch. After coming back my hometown, my wife learned Tajik by herself. Later, due to her outstanding performance, she was sent to work at Xinjiang Normal University and became an official teacher in Confucius Institute after passing the exam. Now I have followed her into the University of Nationalities in Tajikistan and become a Chinese teacher. As a saying goes in China, "A century makes an encounter, a thousand years makes a couple". Sometimes, when I wake up I felt like it was a dream. As my wife is a Chinese, what matters most in our happy life is that both of our hometowns have a long history, and we share great cultural values, good international relations and profound friendship from head to grass root. The ambassador who issued us the marriage certificate said that historical records showed that there was a Chinese princess married in Tajikistan 3,500 years ago.

In 2005, our salary was so low, about $20, that we couldn't afford renting an apartment, let alone buying one. Knowing our situation, the defense secretary authorized a housing allowance of $100 a month for us, saying that as China has given us so much aid, we cannot let our daughter-in-law suffer in Tajikistan. Many times, when he or other military leaders had a visit or reception with Chinese guests, he would proudly introduce me as a Chinese son-in-law to them. At that time, Tajik families were all extended families, with average seven or eight children and all living together. The minister has reminded me for several times that the social situation in China was different from ours, and I must explain to my wife patiently so that she would not be confused by the lifestyle of the extended family. In 2006, I went to China for further study. During that period, my wife was hospitalized and my father died, everything piled up into a mess. But my colleagues and leaders were waiting outside the operating room, sharing the anxiety and pain with us. Everytime I look back, scenes of the past leap before my eyes my wife and I are deeply moved by the fact that we have such a good relationship, which contributes to our happy marriage. From 2010 to 2012, I was in charge of the translation work of the "Officers' Home" building of the Tajik Ministry of National Defense assisted by Chinese Ministry of National Defense. There were Tajik words on the stone tablet of "Officers' Home", which I translated as "Plant a tree of friendship and bear rich fruits".

Many livelihood projects in Tajikistan are funded by Chinese companies or supported by the Chinese government. In the past, Tajikistan was faced with a serious shortage of electricity resources and the electricity supply was time-limited in winter. Since the establishment of Xinjiang TBEA Thermal power plant, it has brought light and warmth to thousands of families. Thus, we don't need to worry about power cutting and can use the water heating system in winter. Road conditions in Tajikistan were not very good. China Road Bridge and Beixin Road Bridge have built several important traffic lines for Tajikistan. The viaduct of the 82 district will soon be completed and opened to traffic. "Tajikistan has changed a lot in the past few years," she said, I replied to her humorously that all of those should attribute to China my second hometown. "Besides, the Tajik people speak highly of Chinese people's spirits of hard-working and toilsome. Now, the Tajik markets have seen the popularity of Chinese products. On one hand, the entering of Chinese products slow down our living costs largely. On the other hand, the settling of Chinese enterprises has improved the employment rate, providing more job opportunities for Tajik people, many of whom were proud to work for Chinese companies. Chinese has been making great changes to China.Not to mention that increasing number off amilies choose to send their children to study in Confucius Institutes. Studying in China has become the dream of more and more young people as Chinese brings our life unexpected changes.

加深乌克兰与中国的合作与关系

［乌克兰］费季切夫・亚历山大
基辅国立语言大学教师

我的中国故事早在1997年就开始了，迄今已经21年。那年我考上了基辅市外国语大学东方语言系，开始学汉语。我的第一位汉语老师是一位中国教授，他姓王，那时候已经60多岁。王老师给我们讲了很多中国

的历史、文化和中国人生活习惯的故事。从此，我对中国就产生了很大的兴趣。

2000 年我第一次去中国，是到北京第二外国语大学留学一年。和现在相比，那时候在中国的外国留学生比较少，特别是来自乌克兰的学生可能在全中国不超过十个人。因此我有更多的机会认识中国朋友，了解中国人的生活方式。我亲眼看到中国改革开放后经济的迅速发展，亲身感受到中国人的热情。那时我是真的爱上了中国。

毕业以后，我留在我的母校当了一名汉语老师。同时我经常做翻译工作，包括陪同乌克兰企业家代表团到中国考察。这样我就有机会亲眼看到中国工业技术从那时候起不断地快速发展。

2005 年乌克兰驻中国大使邀请我到乌克兰驻华大使馆工作。2006 年我成为一名乌克兰驻华大使馆的外交官。由于我会汉语，有做翻译的经验，我的主要工作是陪同大使和乌克兰高级领导，给他们做翻译。这样我有很多机会看到中国最发达的地区，包括上海、深圳等城市，中国最先进的企业，了解中国政府各领域，包括经济、文化、教育、外交等方面的政策。从此，我非常佩服中国政府管理国家的智慧和中国人民勤劳改善生活的精神。

另外，我对中国的外交政策产生了浓厚兴趣。2010 年我离开大使馆回到乌克兰以后，在乌克兰外交部外交学院进修了两年。2012 年我写的毕业论文题目就是“中国现代外交政策”。而最近中国外交政策又有了很大的变化：2013 年习近平主席提出“一带一路”倡议，引起了很多国家的高度关注。目前有很多国家积极参与“丝绸之路经济带”和“21 世纪海上丝绸之路”框架内的基础设施建设项目。这证明，中国在国际舞台上的地位和作用得到显著提高。

2013 年至 2017 年，我在乌克兰驻华大使馆当副领事。这期间我发现越来越多乌克兰人到中国打工，越来越多的乌克兰留学生来中国留学，越来越多的乌克兰人和中国人结婚。由此可见，中国和乌克兰的联系越来越紧密。

我认为，乌克兰一定要进一步加深与中国的合作和关系。我深信，在两国政府和人民共同努力下，通过充分挖掘两国互利合作的潜力，一定能促进两国的经济发展，为两国人民创造更好的生活条件。而我个人愿意为此做出自己的贡献。

To Enhance the Cooperation and Communication between China and Ukraine

Fedichev Oleksandr / Ukraine

Kyiv State Linguistic University, Lecturer

My China story began as early as 1997, and it has been 21 years. In that year I entered the Department of Oriental Languages at Kiev International Studies University and began to learn Chinese. My first Chinese teacher was a Chinese professor, Mr. Wang, who was in his 60s at that time. Mr. Wang told us many stories about Chinese history, culture and Chinese people's living habits. Since then, I have become interested in China.

The first time I went to China was in 2000 because I was accepted to study in Beijing International Studies University. At that time, foreign students were hardly seen in China, with less than ten of them from Ukraine in particular. So I had more chance to make Chinese friends and knew more about their lifestyles. Besides, as I have seen the rapid development of Chinese economy since the reform and opening-up, and have felt the hospitality of Chinese people, I did fall in love with China.

After graduation, I stayed at my Alma school and taught Chinese there. At the same time, I did some translation, including accompanying delegations of Ukrainian entrepreneurs on visits to China. That's how I could have witness the rapid development of industrial technology since then.

In 2005, the Ukrainian ambassador to China invited me to work in the Ukrainian Embassy in China, where I worked as a diplomat at the Ukrainian embassy in China the next year. As I could speak Chinese and had some experience in translation, my main job was to accompany the ambassador and senior Ukrainian leaders and translate for them. In this way, I had many opportunities to see the most developed regions in China, including Shanghai, Shenzhen and other cities, and the most advanced enterprises in China, and learned about the Policies of the Chinese government in various fields, including economy, culture, education and foreign affairs. Since then, I have admired the Chinese government's wisdom in running the country and the Chinese people's spirit of improving their lives through hard work.

In addition, I became very interested in China's foreign policy. After returning to Ukraine from the Embassy in 2010, I studied at the Diplomatic Academy of the Ukrainian Foreign Ministry for two years. The title of my 2012 graduation thesis was "China's Modern Foreign Policy". Recent years have seen the great progress in China's foreign policy. In 2013, President Xi Jinping put forward the "The Belt and Road" initiative, which attracted great attention from many countries. At present, many countries are actively participating in the infrastructure construction projects within the framework of the Silk Road Economic Belt and the 21st Century Maritime Silk Road. This proves that China's status and role in the international arena have been significantly improved.

From 2013 to 2017, I served as vice Consul in the Ukrainian Embassy in China. During this period, I found that an increasing number of Ukrainians came to China to work, to study and many of them got married with Chinese. All of those proved that the interaction between these two countries is getting closer.

I think Ukraine must enhance the cooperation and communication with China. I believe that with the joint efforts of the governments and people of the two countries and by giving full play of the potential in mutually beneficial cooperation, the two countries will promote economic development and create better living conditions for their people. And personally, I would like to make my own contribution to it.

我与中国的奇妙缘分

[突尼斯] 哈利德
迦太基大学突尼斯高等语言学院助理教授

我的英文名字是 Khaled Elhaj Ahmed，中文名字是哈利德，是迦太基大学突尼斯高等语言学院的一名汉语老师。我和中国有缘分，从小心里有中国梦，上大学时，本科专业就是中国语言文学。我越学习汉语，越对中

国语言文化有兴趣。我心里有一个梦，期待哪天有机会去中国，去感受这一神秘的国家。大学四年级时，我参加了汉语桥比赛，表现良好，中国政府给了我去中国学习旅游一个月的机会。我原计划去法国读硕士，不过我到了中国以后，发现一个月的体验完全不够，所以自己申请在成都的西南财经大学进修六个月，同时通过突尼斯高教部申请中国政府奖学金，在北京语言大学攻读硕士学位。

2008 年到 2014 年，我一直在北京学习生活，先后获得了硕士和博士学位。其间，中国也给我带来了幸福。在中国的愉快日子里，我认识了我的妻子，一起开始了我们的新生活。现在我是两个男孩的父亲。我觉得我和中国非常有缘，而且缘分越来越深。

在学业方面，我从中国的老师和同学身上学到了很多。在他们的帮助和鼓励下，我学到了很多知识，汉语水平和学术能力也得到了提高，让我有足够的积累和经验回国当一名汉语老师。在这个基础上，我开始不断深入研究中国文学和文化，撰写了不少学术论文，也参加了许多国际学术会议。我生活的每一步都跟中国有关，我觉得还需要多研究中国不同的领域。作为青年汉学家、翻译家，我会多种语言，觉得自己有责任把中国各个方面的贡献和成就介绍到我的国家，让突尼斯的学者有机会去学习中国的经验。我最近开始从事翻译工作，翻译了几本中国的图书，在突尼斯出版。

在生活方面，在中国的学习生活让我从中国人身上学到了很多。中国人工作很刻苦、很认真。我在中国的时候跟不同地方的中国人相处，他们都会代表自己的家乡给我介绍这个地方的特色。我的这些中国朋友可以说是中国各地的民间大使，通过跟他们的相处和交流也加深了我对中国文化和文明的理解。

我和中国的故事还没完成，中国这一神秘的国家值得我一生研究和学习。我和中国的奇妙缘分还在继续，远远没有结束。我的梦想是在突尼斯传播中国语言文化，给爱学中国语言文化的学生授课，翻译更多的中国名著，这都需要我不断地观察和研究中国各个方面的发展。

My Magic Connection with China

Khaled Elhaj Ahmed / Tunisia

Higher Institute of Languages, Tunis, Carthage University, Assistant Professor

I have a Chinese name, Ha Lide and I'm teaching Chinese at the Higher Institute of Languages of Tunis at the University of Carthage. It is fate that bonded me with China. When I was a child, the love for China was bred in my heart. Besides, my undergraduate major was Chinese language and literature. The more I know Chinese, the more interested I become in Chinese language and culture. I have a dream in my heart, looking forward to the opportunity to go to China one day, to feel this mysterious country. When I was a senior school student in college, I took part in the Chinese Bridge Competition and did well, gaining an opportunity to study and travel in China for one month. Though I originally planned to study for a master's degree in France, when I arrived in China, I found that the one-month experience was not enough. So I applied for a six-month further study in the Southwestern University of Finance and Economics in Chengdu. Meanwhile, I applied for a Chinese government scholarship through the ministry of higher education in Tunisia to study for a master's degree in Beijing Language and Culture University.

From 2008 to 2014, I had lived and studied in Beijing, and had received my master's degree and doctor's degree successively. Meanwhile, China brought me happiness. During that time, I met my wife and started our new life together. Now I'm the father of two boys. Fate brought me with China and I feel like I'm increasingly bonded with China.

Academically, I have learned a lot from my Chinese teachers and classmates. With their help and encouragement, I have gained a lot of knowledge, improved my Chinese and academic ability, which qualified me to be a Chinese teacher back home. On this basis, I began to study Chinese literature and culture in depth, wrote many academic papers, and participated in many international academic conferences. My whole life has been related to China, and I always felt that I needed to study various fields of China. As a young Sinologist and translator, I can speak many languages, and I feel it was my duty to introduce to my country the contributions and achievements of China in various aspects, so that Tunisian scholars can have the opportunity to learn from China. Recently, I started working as a translator and translated several Chinese books which were published in Tunisia.

In terms of life, I have learned a lot from Chinese people when studying in China. They are hard-working and responsible to their work. When I was in China, I got along with Chinese people from different places, and they would introduce the features of this place to me on behalf of their own hometown. In my view, these Chinese friends of mine are just the civil ambassadors from all over China, and through getting along with them, I have deepened my understanding of Chinese culture and civilization.

My story with China is still going forward as China is a mysterious country worth exhausting all my life studying and learning. My magic connection with China continues and it is far from ending. My dream is to spread Chinese language and culture in Tunisia, to teach students who love Chinese language and culture, and to translate more Chinese classics. All of these require me to constantly observe and study the development of China in all aspects.

我的汉语人生

［土耳其］艾国强
穆罕默德·阿基夫·艾尔索伊大学助理研究员

我是来自土耳其的艾国强。艾国强这个名字是我一位中国老师给我起的。虽然有时候一些年轻的中国朋友一听到我的中文名字，就会开玩笑说："这名字太土了吧！还是给你起一个新的名字。"但是我还是很喜欢我的中文名字，因为这个名字伴随我将近 10 年了，已经融入我的生活中。

我是在一座人口不到 1 万人的小镇长大的，那里虽然美丽，但因为地方小，各方面的机会并不多，当时家里的条件一般，当然也没有电脑和网络。别说我们那小地方，连在当时的土耳其大城市网络也不是很普遍。所以在小地方成长的孩子们只能去图书馆写作业、学习、借阅图书。那座规模算不上大的图书馆是我第一次有机会了解中国的地方。在图书馆的书架上有一本名为《中国神话故事》的书，当时立刻引起了我的注意，直到现在那本书还深深留在我的记忆里，我清楚地记得书里面的一些图片，有龙、熊猫、竹林、老虎、长城等。回忆童年，我还记得发生在课堂里的一件事儿，当时我字母写得不漂亮，怎样写老师都不满意，最后老师骂我："臭孩子，你写的字母一点儿不像土耳其语字母，更像中国字！"老师虽然批评了我，但我的内心还是非常快乐！

在土耳其上高中需要选择专业，当时因为我的物理、化学、数学成绩都不好，所以我选择了外语专业。在高中学了 4 年的英语和德语，我在全国统一高考的成绩非常好，当然我父母也特别高兴，他们给亲戚朋友打电话说："我儿子高考成绩特别好，可以考上土耳其最著名大学的英文专业了"。对于这一点，我觉得中国人会非常理解我父母当时的心情，孩子的学习成绩好了，也会让父母在亲戚朋友面前很有面子，对吧？可是，让我父母失望的是：儿子选择了中文专业！家人都反对，我爷爷警告我："小子，你学中文，很可能找不到工作，恐怕找老婆都有困难。"就连最要好的朋友也说我疯了。然而我并没有放弃我的梦想，考上了土耳其法提赫大学的中文系。

大学二年级时，我参加了第八届"汉语桥"世界大学生中文比赛，在

土耳其赛区得了二等奖，中国驻土耳其大使馆给我提供在中国留学两个学期的奖学金。2009 年 8 月 28 日我乘飞机赴中国求学，长途飞行之后，平安抵达北京。这时，我有一种从梦中醒来的惊讶，用讶异的眼光环视四周后，我才真得相信我的梦想已经实现了。虽然那是我第一次去中国，我一点儿都没有感到陌生，好似在自己的国家。那一年是我人生中最难忘的一年，2010 年 7 月，我带着很多美好的回忆踏上了回国旅途。2011 年本科毕业之前，在老师们的鼓励下我再次参加了“汉语桥”比赛（第十届），这次获得了一等奖。

2015 年我得到中国政府奖学金，去了南开大学学习，这一次很幸运的是有我的爱人陪同。这对于我爷爷来说，根本不是他能想到的事儿，他得知这个消息后说：“是因为运气好！”我爱人在南开大学也学了些中文，刚开始她觉得汉语很难学，学不会，但是过了几个月后，我发现她偷偷去淘宝注册账号，并开始购物。我看到她用汉语跟淘宝客服联系解决购物时遇到的问题，我才明白女人只要足够努力，任何目标都可以实现。她为了在淘宝上购物，学会了中文！真让我“害怕”！

2017 年 4 月 10 日，我们两口之家添加了一位新成员！我儿子艾德瑞出生了！正好那天，在南开大学认识的一个好朋友张宁老师到达土耳其。他说：“我相信我跟你儿子很有缘分，他出生的那天我到土耳其来了，如果你们愿意，我想当他的干爸。”我们当然很开心地接受，并请求他给他干儿子起了中文名字。

2018 年，我被“孔子新汉学计划”中外合作培养项目录取，九月又一次到南开大学学习。而这次也有艾德瑞的陪伴，我们拭目以待看看他会不会学点中国话。

My Chinese Life Started from Chinese Language

Aykut Dal / Turkey

Mehmet Akif Ersoy University, Assistant Professor

I'm Ai Guoqiang from Turkey and my Chinese name was given by one of my Chinese teachers. Although sometimes some of my young Chinese friends, when they hear my Chinese name, joke around and say, "That name is too corny! I'll give you a new name." But I still like my Chinese name very much, because this name has been with me for nearly 10 years and has been part of my life.

I grew up in a small town with a population of no more than 10,000. Though it was beautiful, chance was rare as it was a small place. With a general living condition, I have no access to computer and internet. In fact, at that time even in the big cities of Turkey, Internet was not common, let alone in our small town. So children like me had to go to the library to do their homework, study and borrow books. Thus, that middle-scaled library was the first place that I had opportunity to learn about China. On the shelf of the library, there was a book named *Chinese Mythological Stories*, which immediately caught my attention. Until now, the book is still deeply in my memory. I still remember clearly some pictures in the book, including dragons, pandas, bamboo forests, tigers, the Great Wall and so on. Recalling the days of my childhood, I still remember one thing happened in class. At that time as my handwriting was not beautiful, the teacher was not satisfied with it no matter how I try to do it better. Finally the teacher scolded me: "Brat! The letters you write are not like Turkish letters at all. They are more like Chinese characters!" Though been criticized, I was very happy!

In Turkey, we need to choose a major, and I choose foreign languages as my major, because of my poor performance in physics, chemistry and mathematics. After four-year study of English and German in the high school, I got good grades in the National College Entrance Examination, which made my parents so pleased that they called and shared this good news to their relatives and friends, "My son has done very well in the college entrance examination, so he can be admitted to study the English major in the most famous university in Turkey". I think it's easy to be understood by Chinese that parents will be very proud of their kids if they have good academic performance. However, what disappointed them was that I chose Chinese as my major. At that time, all my families were opposed to my decision and my grandparent even warned me: "my boy, if you study Chinese, you probably won't get a job. I'm afraid you'll have trouble finding a wife." Even my closest friends called me crazy boy. However, I did not give up my dream and was admitted to the Chinese Department of Fatih University in Turkey.

When I was a sophomore, I took part in the 8th "Chinese Bridge" Chinese Proficiency Competition for Foreign College Students and won the second prize in the Turkish region. The Chinese embassy in Turkey offered me a scholarship to study in China for two semesters. On August 28, 2009, I took a plane to China to study, after a long journey, arrived in Beijing safely. At that time, I was surprised as if I came to the wonderland in my dream. I looked around in amazement before truly believing my dream has come true. Although it was my first time to China, I felt familiar with it, as if it's my own country. That year was the most memorable one in my life. In July 2010, I set foot on the journey back to China with many wonderful memories.Before my graduation in 2011, with the encouragement of my teachers, I made up my mind to participate in the 10th "Chinese Bridge" Competition and won the first prize at that time.

In 2015, I got the Chinese government scholarship and went to Nankai University to study for two semesters. This time, I was very lucky to be accompanied by my wife. For my grandfather, this was not what he had expected at all. When he heard the news, he said, "It was just luck!" My wife also learned some Chinese in Nankai University. At first, she thought it was difficult to learn Chinese, but a few months later, I found that she secretly registered an account on Taobao and started shopping. Once I saw her talking to Taobao's customer service center in Chinese to solve her shopping problems, I realized that a woman can achieve any goal if she works hard enough. She learned Chinese in order to shop on Taobao! How crazy she was!

On April 10, 2017, we had a new family member that was my son! On that day, one of my good friends in Nankai University, Mr. Zhang Ning arrived in Turkey. He said, "If you like, I want to be his godfather." Of course, we were happy to accept and asked him to give his godson a Chinese name.

This year, I was admitted to the Sino-foreign cooperative training program of "Confucius Studies Program", and I will study in Nankai University again in September. We'll see if can pick up some Chinese as he came here with us this time.

了解中国、研究中国政治制度、改善中美关系

[美国] 胡瑞雪
宾夕法尼亚大学博士生

我在美国的一个小镇长大，我大学的专业是美国政治。简而言之，在上大学之前我很少关注国际新闻，但我经常了解美国国内新闻，在那时我对中国的了解不深。

现在我为什么研究中美关系呢？当我住在纽约的时候，我有位朋友给我介绍中国的文化。他和家人从上海移民到了美国。他奶奶不会英语，我没办法跟他的奶奶用同一种语言聊天，但是我发现了中文的美丽。对我来说，听人说中文简直像听音乐，看人写汉字好像是欣赏艺术，然后我就决定学习这门迷人的语言。我的朋友给我带来新的体验使我大开眼界，了解中国成了我的爱好。在我看来，没有比学习中国文化更有意思，我也喜欢上中国文化并开始学习中文。去北京旅行的时候，我发现北京的建筑新颖别致，随处可见具有创造力和现代化的建筑。我也发现北京拥有古老的历史，在北海公园看到的传统舞蹈让我体会到中国文化的古典美，这让我印象深刻。

在这之后，我开始关注中国的政治，在学习中国文化上投入很多精力。为了学习中美关系，我申请到哥伦比亚研究所学习。在某种程度上，在美国学习中文不容易，然而哥伦比亚研究所提供了许多学习中国历史和时事的机会。作为研究生，我能拿到奖学金去北京学习中文，我感到非常高兴。

现在我开始博士阶段学习，我的专业是国际关系，我的研究方向是中国的网络安全。在这次上海之旅后我想学习中国的网络安全法。随着科技的发展，信息媒体的问题越来越多，我们怎么控制快速发展的科技和网络安全是一个问题。我想比较中美两个国家在处理网络安全上的不同和优缺点。我想了解中国的政府是怎么利用法律，保障网络安全，维护社会公共秩序。

习近平主席说，“在新的历史时期，中国梦的本质是国家富强、人民幸福”。我希望我能越来越了解中国，更好地研究中国的政治制度，为改善中美关系做出努力。我感谢中国政府的邀请，给我那么棒的机会了解并学习新的文化。

Learning China, Studying Chinese Political System and Improving China-US Relations

Rachel Ann Hulvey / United States of America

Ph.D.student, University of Pennsylvania

I grew up in a small town in America, and majored in American politics in college. In short, I paid little attention to international news before I went to college. Of course, I didn't know much about China at that time, but I often read domestic newspapers.

Now why do I study Sino-US relations? When I lived in New York, one of my friends gave me an introduction of Chinese culture. His family used to live in Shanghai and immigrated to the United States. His grandma cannot speak English. Though, I couldn't talk to his grandma in the same language, I found the beauty of Chinese. To me, listening to spoken Chinese is like listening to music, and watching people write Chinese characters gives me a sense of appreciating an art. Then I decided to learn this charming language. New experiences brought by my friends widen my horizon, so I began to find what I love. In my opinion, there is nothing more interesting than learning Chinese culture. I fell in love with Chinese culture and began to learn Chinese. On my travel to Beijing, I found the architectures there were really novel, creative and modern. Besides, I found that Beijing was a city with a long history. I can see traditional dance in Beihai Park which made me feel the classical beauty of Chinese culture, and impressed me deeply.

From then on, I started to pay attention to Chinese politics and bent efforts to learn Chinese culture. In order to study Sino-American relations, I applied to the Columbia Institute of Studies. To some extent, it was not easy to learn Chinese in the United States, but Columbia Institute offered many opportunities to learn Chinese history and current affairs. As a graduate student, I was very happy and grateful that I can get a scholarship to study Chinese in Beijing.

Now I am starting my doctoral study, my major is international relations, and my research direction is Chinese network security. During this trip to Shanghai, I want to learn about Chinese cyber security law. With the development of science and technology, there are an increasingly number of problems in information media.How to balance the rapid development of science and technology and network security is what we should pay more attention to. I think by comparing the differences, advantages and disadvantages between China and the United States in dealing with cyber security and I want to know how the Chinese government makes full use of laws to ensure cyber security and maintain social and public order.

President Xi Jinping said, “In this new historical era, the Chinese dream that we are pursuing is about the economic prosperity of the country and happiness of the people.” I hope I can learn more about China, have a better study of its political system, and make efforts to improve China-US relations. I am grateful to the Chinese government for inviting me and giving me such a great opportunity to learn about a new culture.

我的三位启蒙老师

［日本］阿部沙织
立命馆大学 语言教育中心 汉语讲师

很荣幸这次能够参加青年汉学家研修计划。我曾经在天津、北京留过学，之后在北京工作过。在中国生活的时间一共有六年多，所以我的中国故事有很多，今天我想讲讲我初识中国的故事。其实，与其说是我的中国故事，不如说是我启蒙老师的故事。我给大家介绍一下我的三位启蒙老师，通过我跟这三位老师的学习经历谈谈我的中国故事。

我出生于 1979 年，也就是中国改革开放的第二年。由于小时候在日本媒体里面很少看到中国的有关消息，所以我对中国没有特别具体的印象。当然和其他小朋友一样，我小时候读过《西游记》，上中学的时候读过鲁迅先生的《阿 Q 正传》和《故乡》，也学过中国历史，但对真实的中国还是一无所知。高三时我选修了汉语课，但那完全是出于对非英语外语的好奇和逃离英语学习压力的想法。没想到，因为上了这门课，我和中国结下了不解之缘。

我从十七岁开始学习汉语，在日本京都的一所不知名的高中读高三。班主任加藤诚是我们的汉语老师。他平时教我们语文，但同时也是个汉语专家。后来我得知，他当高中老师之前是一直研究中国文学的。我们当时只知道他会说汉语，当我们班主任之前曾经在中国教过日语。

一周一节的汉语课，难度并不高，老师好像更注重让我们接触当代中国文化，让我们听听中国歌曲，看看中国新闻节目、中国电影。我在不知不觉中被汉语美丽的旋律所吸引，最后被陈凯歌的《霸王别姬》、王家卫的《阿飞正传》迷住了。后来我放弃高考复习，天天听中国流行歌曲，有时间就去租中国电影的录像带，通过那些大众文化慢慢接触到中国当代文化。

加藤老师后来从我们高中退休，从 2007—2017 年一直在西安外国语大学教日语，同时担任京都地区日中友好协会的常任理事。现在我才明白，原来我的启蒙老师是一位隐形的中国专家，他潜移默化地教我们汉语以及中国文化，这种让年轻的我们直接接触中国当代文化的教学方式，现在想来可能源于他对中国文化的敬佩和信任，因为他知道我们一旦接触中国文化就会被打动。后来我在北京工作时，他对我说过一句话，我铭记至

今。他说："请尊重你的中国同事和他们的工作，同时必须要做一个被中国同事尊重的日本人。"在北京工作的一年里，我深感他此话的含义。人和人之间，尤其是具有不同文化习惯的人之间，应该学会互相理解、互相尊重。跟加藤老师学了一年汉语后，我考上了早稻田大学，在这里我遇到了我的第二位启蒙老师：铃木康雄。铃木康雄老师当时虽已年届七旬，但却很有魅力，他对教学的热情不同寻常。他对一些发音不准的同学非常严厉，大声批评发音不达标。刚上大学的我们都很敬畏这位老师，但时间久了，慢慢知道铃木老师的这些做法都出于对我们的期待。有时课间他会和我们讲讲他的生平，他是跟随他的父亲——汉语言学者铃木择郎先生在上海度过他的幼年。他告诉我们，他小时候还被鲁迅先生摸过头呢。他对中国的感情很深，说到汉语，对他来说就是第二母语，所以教学才那么严谨。他在上海就读于东亚同文书院——日本人于清末创办的一所私立大学，1945 年因日本投降他辍学回国，后来到一个电器厂做了四十年销售。他说："即使是你不愿做的工作，既然入了行就要做到底，毕竟功夫不负有心人嘛"。他回国后的生活可能有种种不易，但并没直接和我们说过。

退休后应在上海读书时的同学推荐，铃木老师开始踏上汉语教师之路，也许那是他的第二个"青春期"，所以他那么热心地面对学生，充满活力地教导我们。大二时我曾到南开大学留学，当时铃木老师非常关心我，还趁同学聚会时到天津看我。我都忘了当时跟铃木老师谈了些什么，只记得在餐厅他对旁边的陌生人说，"我是在上海长大的"，那样铿锵有力的声音和喜形于色的表情，说明中国对他来说是第二个家乡。万万没想到的是，铃木老师三年后就辞世了。后来我和铃木老师一样在大学当汉语教师，经常自问：我对学生有像铃木老师那样的热心吗？为什么不能像铃木老师那样对学生保持严厉的态度？铃木老师热爱中国，因为中国是养育他的第二故乡。他那种既爱中国，又逃不出对自我身份的矛盾，体现在他教学时的激烈感情。但这只是我的猜测，他自己从没对我们讲过他的想法。他对我们汉语的要求表现在他对中国语言文化的崇高敬意。

留学回来后，我遇到的第三位启蒙老师也姓铃木——早稻田大学日语研究中心的铃木义昭教授。我本科读的是日本文学专业，并没有正式学过中国文学这门课，回国后选修中日对照语言学，担任这门课的老师就是铃木教授。他是研究闻一多的专家，20 世纪 80 年代末作为日语专家到北京大学教学。班里有很多他的研究生，日本人和中国人各有一半。我很喜欢铃木教授课上国际化的气氛。他很豪爽，期末时让我们本科学生也到他的办公室，举办小小的宴会。他的办公室四面都是书，关于日语教学和中国文学的。在那儿中日学生有时用日语有时用汉语谈论各种话题，气氛很和谐，又充满着对学习和未来的激情。铃木先生那时建议我继续学习中文，也鼓励我转学中国文学专业。我当时对未来很迷惘，由于日本经济很不景气，我去过几家公司的招聘面试都没通过，在考虑读研。最后还是铃木先生的鼓励让我下定决心，第二年我踏上了研究中国文学之路。所以，铃木先生是我的中国文学的启蒙老师。我成为御茶水女子大学的研究生以后，还经常拜访铃木先生，他用王瑶先生的《中国新文学史稿》给我讲授文学史。后来通过铃木教授的介绍，我有幸跟北京大学中文系商金林教授进修了两年。很可惜，铃木教授去年突然离开了人世。他退休时把大量藏书赠送给北京大学东方系和山西博物馆等中国研究机构。希望铃木老师的这些“遗产”能够有助于培养出下一代的中国研究者。

以上我谈到的三位启蒙老师，他们的共同特点是对中国有着无限的热爱和尊重。虽说中国和日本自古以来是一衣带水的邻邦，但近代两国之间有一段不幸的历史——日本的侵略战争给中国带来了极大的伤害和灾难。因此，受历史影响，中日关系至今还很微妙，时好时坏，两国人民对对方的感情也很矛盾。所以，中日两国的关系很特殊，我想，尤其我们日本人作为过去的侵略者，需要努力描绘未来中日关系的美好蓝图。六年的中国生活和这几年在日本的教学经验，我发现彼此缺乏对对方的理解。构建友好关系首先需要了解对方，了解对方才能够欣赏、尊重对方之美。我想我们做汉学研究的，有责任给年轻一代推广关于中国国情和文化知识。我谈到的这三位老师，都想尽各种方法让学生接触中国的方方面面，而且都很渴望让我们更好地了解中国。我好像被命运指引一样，也步入做中文教师的行列。至今我带过一千多名学生，但至于我是否会像我的三位启蒙老师那样很好地展示中国文化之深奥和伟大，我还没有足够信心。但我的目标很明确，我要用一辈子来努力做一个像我的恩师们那样的教师，以便更好地培养下一代，构建中日美好的未来。

My Enlightenment Teachers

Abe Saori / Japan

Ritsumeikan University, Language Education Centre, Chinese Lecturer

It is my great honor to participate in the Visiting Program for Young Sinologists. I have studied in Tianjin, and Beijing and once worked in Beijing. Altogether, I have stayed in China for more than six years, so I have experienced a lot in China. Now, I want to share them with you. In fact, they're more about stories happened between me and my enlightenment teachers than my experiences in China. Then, I would like to introduce to you three of my enlightenment teachers. Through sharing my learning experiences with these three teachers, you'll have a better understanding of my China story.

I was born in 1979, the second year of China's reform and opening up. Since I seldom read about China in Japanese media when I was a child, I had no specific impression of China. Of course, like other children, I read *Journey to the West* when I was a child. In middle school, I read *The True Story of Ah Q* and *My Hometown* written by Lu Xun. I also studied Chinese history, but I still knew nothing about real China. In my third year of high school, I could take Chinese as a selective course, but I decided to start learning Chinese was out of curiosity for non-English foreign languages and the desire to escape from the pressure of English study. Unexpectedly, because of this course, I formed an indissoluble bond with China.

I began to learn Chinese when I was in 17 years old being a senior three student in an unknown high school in Kyoto, Japan. The head teacher, Kato

Cheng, was our Chinese teacher. He taught us Chinese, and he was also an expert in this field. Later, I knew he had been studying Chinese literature before he became a high school teacher. All we knew at that time was that he could speak Chinese and that he had taught Japanese in China before being our class teacher.

We had the Chinese class once a week, which was not very difficult. The teacher seemed to focus more on letting us get in touch with contemporary Chinese culture, listening to Chinese songs, watching Chinese news programs and movies. I was attracted by the beautiful melody of Chinese unconsciously, and finally was absorbed by Chen Kaige's *Farewell My Concubine* and Wong Kar-wai's *Days of Being Wild*. Later, I gave up studying for the college entrance examination and immersed in listening Chinese pop songs every day. I would rent videos of Chinese movies whenever I had time, and gradually came into contact with the contemporary Chinese culture through the mass culture.

Mr. Kato later retired from our high school and was teaching Japanese at Xi'an International Studies University from 2007 to 2017. He also served as a permanent director of the Japan-China Friendship Association in Kyoto Region. Now, I can understand that my enlightenment teacher is a China expert who exerts a subtle influence of Chinese and Chinese culture on us. The teaching way that the young can direct contact with the Chinese contemporary culture. It may have originated from his admiration and trust of the Chinese culture, because he knew that once we contact with the Chinese culture we will enamored of it. Later, when I started working in Beijing, he said something to me that I still remember. "Please respect your Chinese colleagues and their work," he said, "meanwhile be respectable." During the year I worked in Beijing, I had a deep understanding of his inner meaning. In terms of personal communication, People, especially those with different cultural habits, should learn to understand and respect each other. After a year of studying Chinese with Mr. Kato, I was admitted to Waseda University, where I met my second enlightenment teacher, Yasuo Suzuki who was then in his seventies, but he was enterprising, and had enormous passion to teaching. He was very strict with some students who did not pronounce well, loudly criticizing them for not being up to standard. When we just went to university, we were almost overwhelmed by the teacher's anger, but as time passed, we gradually knew that what he did were out of expectation for us. Sometimes during the break, he would tell us about his life. He spent his childhood in Shanghai with his father, Mr. Shiroo Suzuki, a Chinese scholar. He told us that Mr. Lu Xun had groped him when he was a child. He had a deep affection for China. Chinese is his second language, which is why he was so rigorous in teaching. He attended the East Asian Tongwen Academy in Shanghai, a private university founded by the Japanese at the end of the Qing Dynasty. He dropped out after the Japanese surrender in 1945 and went back to China to work as a salesman in an electrical appliance factory for 40 years. He said, "Even if it's a job you don't want to do, you have to stick it out. After all, where there's a will, there's a way". He must has gone through twists and turns after backing Japan, but he seldom complain to us.

After he retired, Mr. Suzuki started to teach Chinese at the recommendation of his classmates in Shanghai. Perhaps he found the feeling of adolescence again, which was the reason why he was so enthusiastic about his students and taught us with great energy. When I studied abroad at Nankai University in my sophomore year, Mr. Suzuki was very concerned about me and even visited me in Tianjin during a class reunion. I don't remember what I talked to him about, except that he said to a stranger in the restaurant, "I grew up in Shanghai," with such a strong voice and a joyful expression, indicating that China was the second home to him. It was totally unexpected that Mr. Suzuki passed away three years later. Then I became a Chinese teacher at the university, just like Mr. Suzuki. I often asked myself: Do I have injected so much enthusiasm for my students as Mr. Suzuki? Why can't I be as strict with my students as Mr. Suzuki was? Mr. Suzuki loves China because it is his second homeland. And he could grow up in Shanghai due to the Japanese invasion of China, so he could do nothing about stopping his studies halfway at the end of the war. His ambivalence about his love for China and his inability to escape his self-identity is reflected in his passion in teaching. But this is only my speculation, he himself never told us what he thought. His high respect for Chinese language and culture was manifested in his demand for us in learning Chinese.

After I returned from studying abroad, I met my third teacher, also named Suzuki--Yoshiaki Suzuki, a Professor of Waseda University Japanese Language Research Center. I studied Japanese literature as an undergraduate but did not formally take Chinese literature class, so when I returned to Japan and took Sino-Japanese Linguistics, Professor Suzuki was my teacher. He was an expert on Wen Yiduo and came to Peking University in the late 1980s to teach as a Japanese language expert. There were many of his graduate students in the class, half Japanese and half Chinese. I liked the international atmosphere of Professor Suzuki's class. He was so generous that he let us undergraduate students come to his office at the end of the semester and held little parties.His office was surrounded by books on Japanese teaching and Chinese literature. There the Chinese and Japanese students sometimes talked about various topics in Japanese and sometimes in Chinese, and the atmosphere was harmonious, and full of enthusiasm for learning and the future. At that time, Mr. Suzuki suggested me to continue studying Chinese and encouraged me to change my major to Chinese literature. I was very confused about my future. Due to the economic downturn in Japan, I had failed several job interviews and was considering furthering my studies in graduate school. In the end, it was Mr. Suzuki's encouragement that made me make up my mind to do it, and the following year I start the journey of studying Chinese literature. So, Mr. Suzuki was my enlightenment teacher of Chinese literature. After I became a graduate student at Ochanomizu Women's University, I often visited Mr. Suzuki, and he taught me the history of literature using Mr. Wang Yao's *The Draft of Modern Chinese Literature History*. Later, through Professor Suzuki's introduction, I had the honor of studying with Professor Shang Jinlin of the Chinese Department of Peking University for two years. Sadly, Professor Suzuki passed away suddenly last year. When he retired, he gave a large collection of books to the Oriental Department of Peking University and the Shanxi Museum and other Chinese research institutions. I hope that these "legacies" of Mr. Suzuki will be helpful to nourish more Chinese researchers

The three enlightenment teachers I have mentioned above have the same infinite love and respect for China. Although China and Japan have been neighbors since ancient times, there is an unfortunate history between the two countries in recent times--the war of aggression against china, which brought great harm and disaster to China. Therefore, influenced by the history, the relationship between China and Japan is still very delicate, sometimes good and sometimes bad, and the two peoples have conflicting feelings towards each other. Therefore, the relationship between China and Japan is very special, and I think that especially we Japanese, as the aggressors of the past, need to work hard to draw a better blueprint for future Sino-Japanese relations. After six years living in China and teaching in Japan during these years, I found that there is a lack of understanding of each other. Building friendly relations requires mutual-understanding in the first place so that we can appreciate and respect the beauty of each other. I think it is our responsibility as sinology researchers to promote knowledge about the Chinese state and culture to the younger generation. The three teachers I mentioned above have tried every possible way to expose their students to all aspects of China, and they are all eager to make us understand China better. As if by fate, I have stepped into the role of a Chinese teacher. I have taught over a thousand students so far, but I am not yet confident that I will be able to demonstrate the depth and greatness of Chinese culture as well as my three enlightenment teachers did. But my goal is clear: I want to devote my life to being a teacher like my mentors, so that I can better nurture the next generation and build a better future for China and Japan. This training program is a great opportunity for me to achieve this goal.

我与中国的缘分

［印度］爱德
贾瓦哈拉尔・尼赫鲁大学研究学者

我叫爱德，来自印度，目前在印度尼赫鲁大学读博士，专业是汉语言文学。今天很荣幸和大家分享我的中国故事，也可以说是我本人跟中国的缘分。我来自印度——一个人口多、社会竞争压力大的国家，印度的父母

就像中国父母一样望子成龙。高中毕业之后我父母建议我学工科，可是我本人对科学一点兴趣都没有，更想学一门外语。那时候，我的一个当记者的舅舅给我提了个建议，他说如果学外语的话最好是选择中文，因为未来中国和印度的崛起，将会给年轻人提供很多机会。幸运的是我被印度最著名的大学——尼赫鲁大学中文系录取了。刚开始学汉语的时候压力真的很大，可是过了一段时间我就爱上了这门语言。俗话说："只要功夫深，铁杵磨成针。"不断的努力和老师们的帮助使我对中国文化、文学、民俗等领域产生浓厚的兴趣。

2013 年我第一次有机会踏上这片土地，那时我到湖南长沙参加"汉语桥"比赛。虽然在中国只待了两个礼拜，可是我深受中国人民的友好对待，舍不得离开中国。回国之后我更加努力学习，2014 年获得了印度教育部的奖学金，到北京语言大学读书。在北语读书的一年当中，我的汉语水平得到了突飞猛进的提高，我学会了有关中国文化、民俗、地理等方面的知识，最关键的是我通过课外活动和周围环境掌握了许多课本上根本学不到的知识。俗话说："读万卷书，行万里路。"在中国读书期间我经常跟朋友去旅行，去了西安、太原、郑州、洛阳、济南、保定、石家庄、呼和浩特、成都、长沙、上海、苏州、杭州等地方。我个人觉得，在中国旅游非常方便，中国人非常友好。我觉得作为一个学习中文的留学生，在中国旅游的最好的方法是坐普通火车，最好坐硬座，这样有更多机会跟老百姓交流，提高自己的中文水平。另外，每次到一个旅游城市最好住青年旅舍，在青年旅舍有更多跟青年人互相交谈、交换意见的机会。

2015 年，我从北语毕业之后，依依不舍地离开了北京，回印度继续读硕士。那时候我在印度天天都想念北京，想念中国，天天祈祷让我回到美丽的中国。2016 年，我获得了中国商务部的奖学金，到了中国人民大学读书。"白日依山尽，黄河入海流。欲穷千里目，更上一层楼"。为了开阔我的视野和对中国的了解，我跨专业选了国际关系，一年当中收获不少。

中印两国都是文明古国，是以佛教为基础的友好邻国。两国之间的文化交流也有着非常悠久的历史。如果我们看古代历史，公元四世纪，法显作为中国第一位到海外取经求法的大师到印度，不仅仅翻译了很多佛经，而且记录了当时天竺国的各种情况。公元五世纪的时候，南印度的一位和尚菩提达摩到了中国，在少林寺创立了禅宗佛教。公元六世纪的时候唐代高僧玄奘到印度取经，不仅为中国的佛教文化做出了卓越贡献，同时还为中印两国人民的文化交流奠定了坚实的基础。明朝的时候，郑和率领两百多艘海船、2.7 万多人下西洋，经过了南印度，同时跟当地的国王和百姓开展交流。如果我们看近代历史，印度诗翁泰戈尔一生三次访问了中国，在不同场合表示了对中国文化的喜爱以及对中华民族的尊重。他的作品对当时的中国文人，比如冰心、徐志摩、陈独秀、胡适、郭沫若等，有着非常深刻的影响。1938 年印度医生柯棣华随同印度援华医疗队到中国协助抗日，先后在延安和华北抗日根据地服务，1942 年他在河北逝世，毛主席为了纪念他，亲笔写了挽词。新中国成立后，中国政府在石家庄建立了柯棣华纪念馆。这些人物对中印两国的友谊做出了非常伟大的贡献。我希望在未来的时间里，通过自己也为中印两国交流做出一些贡献。希望在未来的时间里，中印两国共同发展、求同存异。“中印友好”、“龙象共舞”是亚洲之幸、世界之福。

My Fate with China

Aditya Kumar Pandey / India
Jawaharlal Nehru University, Research Scholar

My name is Ade from India. Now I am studying for a Ph.D at Nehru University in India, majoring in Chinese language and literature. Today I am honored to share my stories with you. It can also be said that it is my fate with China. I come from India, a country with a large population and high social competition. Indian parents are like Chinese parents hoping their children will have a bright future. After graduating from high school, my parents suggested that I study engineering, but I have no interest in it at all, and prefer to learn a foreign language. At that time, one of my uncles who was a reporter gave me a suggestion. He said that if you learn a foreign language, it will be best to choose Chinese, because the rise of China and India in the future will provide many opportunities for young people. Fortunately, I was admitted to the Chinese Department of Nehru University, the most famous university in India. When I first started learning Chinese, it was really stressful, but after a while I fell in love with the language. As the saying goes: "As long as you work hard, you can grind an iron pestle into a needle." Constant efforts and the help of teachers have made me interested in Chinese culture, literature, folklore and other fields.

I had the first opportunity to set foot on this land in 2013, when I went to Changsha, Hunan to participate in the Chinese Bridge Competition. Although I only stayed in China for two weeks, I was treated very friendly by the Chinese people and I was reluctant to leave China. After returning India, I studied harder.

In 2014, I received a scholarship from the Ministry of Education of India to study at the famous Beijing Language and Culture University. During a year of studying there, my Chinese has been improved by leaps and bounds. I have learned about Chinese culture, folklore, geography, etc. The most important thing is that I have learned a lot that are unavailable in many textbooks through extracurricular activities and the surrounding environment. As the saying goes: "Read thousands of books, travel thousands of miles." During my studies in China, I often traveled with friends to Xi'an in Shaanxi, Taiyuan in Shanxi, Zhengzhou in Henan, Luoyang, Jinan in Shandong, Baoding in Hebei, Shijiazhuang, Hohhot in Inner Mongolia, and Sichuan. Chengdu, Changsha, Hunan, Shanghai, Suzhou, Hangzhou and other places. I personally think that traveling in China is very convenient and the Chinese are very friendly. I think as an international student studying Chinese, the best way to travel in China is to take an ordinary train, preferably a hard seat, so that you have more opportunities to communicate with the people and improve your Chinese level. In addition, every time you go to a city for traveling, it is better to live in a youth hostel, where there are more opportunities to discuss and exchange opinions with young people.

In 2015, after graduating from Beijing Language and Culture University, I reluctantly left Beijing and returned to India to continue my master's study. Recalling those days, I remembered that, I missed Beijing and China every day, and I begged God to let me return to beautiful China. In 2016, I received a scholarship from the Ministry of Commerce of China and went to study at Renmin University of China. There is a poem written by a famous Chinese poet Wang Zhihuan: "The sun beyond the mountain glows; The Yellow River seawards flows. You can enjoy a grander sight; By climbing to a greater height." In order to broaden my horizons and deepen my understanding of China, I chose International Relations as my trans-disciplinary major and gained a lot during the year.

Both China and India are ancient civilizations and friendly neighbors based on Buddhism. The cultural exchanges between the two countries also have a very long history. Looking back at ancient history, we can see that in the fourth century AD, Faxian who has never gone to India was the first man that had gone on a pilgrimage for Buddhist script and the truth. He not only translated many Buddhist scriptures, but also recorded various situations in the India at that time. In the fifth century AD, Bodhidharma, a monk from South India, came to China and founded Zen Buddhism in Shaolin Temple. In the sixth century AD, Tang Priest, an eminent monk in the Tang Dynasty, went to India to get the scriptures. He not only made outstanding contributions to Chinese Buddhist culture, but also laid a solid foundation for cultural exchanges between the Chinese and Indian people. During the Ming Dynasty, Zheng He led more than 200 ships withmore than 27,000 people to the West, passing through South India, and at the same time communicated with local kings and ordinary people. If we look at modern history, Indian poet Tagore visited China three times in his life and expressed his love for Chinese culture and respect for the Chinese nation on different occasions. His works had a very profound influence on Chinese literati at the time, such as Bing Xin, Xu Zhimo, Chen Duxiu, Hu Shi, Guo Moruo, etc. In 1938, Indian doctor Ke Dihua accompanied the Indian medical team to China to assist in the resistance against Japan. He served successively in Yan'an and the North China Anti-Japanese Base. In 1942, he died in Hebei. Chairman Mao Zedong sent an autograph to commemorate him. After the founding of New China in 1945, the Chinese government established the Ke Dihua Memorial Hall in Shijiazhuang, Hebei. These characters have made a great contribution to the friendship between China and India. I hope that in the future, I will make some contributions to the exchanges between China and India through giving full play of my language skill. I hope that in the future, China and India will develop together and seek common ground while reserving differences. “China-India friendship” and “dragon and elephant dancing together” are the blessings of Asia and the world.

我与汉语教学

［乌克兰］卡丽娜
基辅国立语言大学高级讲师

说起我的中国故事，应该可以追溯到20世纪80年代末。1989年2月，我妈妈到中国旅行，当时正好是中国的春节假期。回国以后，妈妈给我讲述了上海、苏州和杭州的美景、中国人庆祝春节的传统习俗以及中国

朋友们的热情接待。从那时起，“中国”——这个遥远而又亲切的名字，就进入了我的心里。也是从那时开始，我与中国就“结缘”了。高中毕业以后，我哥哥劝我说：“你一定要学汉语，中国是最有前途的国家，汉语将成为最受欢迎的语言！”因此，1995 年上大学时，我选择了中文专业，踏上了自己的汉语之路。这样我就开始实现我和家庭的梦想。

在攻读本科学位的那段时间里，我积极参加学校安排的各种课外活动，还参加了全乌克兰大学生中文比赛，并获第三名，所以 1999 年我获得了中国政府奖学金，在浙江大学进修了一年。那一年，我不仅提高了汉语水平，体验了丰富的校园生活和多彩的风俗美景，还更深入了解了中国的悠久历史、文化和传统习俗，感受到中国人民的好客和爱心。那一年，我就完全爱上了中国。

回乌克兰以后，我的唯一理想是当中文老师，帮助更多的人了解这个特别有意思的、迷人的、难忘的中国历史、文化和语言世界。毕业之后，我开始在基辅国立语言大学教中文。在课堂上，我尽可能让学生们感受中文的美丽和深度，支持他们自主策划和中国文化和传统假期有关的各种活动。我希望他们虽然还没亲眼看到，但是通过我讲述的故事能够想象出中国；我不但教他们中文，还要把我对中国的热爱教给他们，让他们爱上我所爱的中国。

2003 年，我获得了中国政府奖学金来中国攻读博士研究生。我先后在中国学习了 8 年时间，在这段时间里，我积极参加学校组织的活动，多次在留学生晚会上表演节目，还喜欢到中国各地旅行。2008 年，我从复旦大学汉语言文字学专业博士毕业后，还组建了自己的幸福家庭，成为母亲。简而言之，中国实现了我心里所梦想的、人生中最重要的事。

回国以后，我来到基辅国立语言大学工作，继续培养乌克兰的汉语人才，发展乌克兰的汉学。同时，我也成为基辅国立语言大学孔子学院学员友谊联合会的指导教师，积极支持、参加孔子学院的各种活动，有时还会带上孩子们一起加入。与孔子学院教师一起包粽子、尝美食，体验端午节日文化。2018 年 2 月，在孔子学院和基辅市敬老院联合举办的“文化的温度”为主题的 2018 年新春联欢晚会上，我和中国教师董雪松用中文、俄语合唱了经典歌曲《红莓花儿开》，为老人们送去新年祝福。最近，我一直在想怎么能够更好地发展乌克兰汉学，所以我积极参与国际合作项目。2017 年，我再次回到中国，受邀参加了上海大学“一带一路”高级研修班，想更深入地了解乌克兰汉学在“一带一路”倡议的发展前途。

另外，我和我家人从未中断与中国的联系。我的三个孩子每天都看很多中国画书，听我给他们讲中国故事。我们夫妻俩很支持小孩学习汉语，每周末送他们到孔子学院少儿汉语班学习汉语，并参加孔子学院安排的各种活动，让他们对中国越来越感兴趣。值得一提的是，孔子学院一位教师给我的三个孩子分别取了中文名：代格巧、代格菲和代格俊，希望我们一家与中国的缘分正如孩子们的名字一样“代代相传”。

总之，谈到我对中国的感情，可以用我曾经演唱过的《大中国》的歌词来表达：“中国，我爱你，你永远在我心里！”从我妈妈给我讲的中国春节的故事到现在，再到未来，我的心、我的灵魂和我的家永远离不开中国!

Chinese Language Teaching and I

Gevorgian Karina / Ukraine

Kyiv National Linguistic University, Senior Lecturer

Speaking of my stories in China, it will go back to the end of the 1980s. In February 1989, my mother traveled to China, which happened to be the Chinese New Year holiday. After returning home, my mother told me about the beautiful scenery of Shanghai, Suzhou and Hangzhou, the traditional customs of Chinese people celebrating the Spring Festival, and the warm reception she received from the Chinese. Since then, "China"--this remote and friendly country, has left in my heart. And just at that time, I have "made a bond" with China. After graduating from high school, my brother persuaded me: "You must learn Chinese. China is the most promising country and Chinese will become the most popular language!" Therefore, when I went to university in 1995, I chose Chinese as a major and started my Chinese learning journey. That was how I began to realize my dreams and my families'.

During the time I was studying for an undergraduate degree, I actively participated in various extracurricular activities arranged by our school. I also participated in the Chinese Language Competition for University Students in Ukraine and won the third place. In 1999, I won a Chinese government scholarship. And had a chance to study at Zhejiang University for a year. In that year, I not only improved my Chinese, experienced the rich campus life and enjoyed colorful customs and scenery, but also got a deeper understanding of China's long history, culture and traditional customs, and felt the hospitality and kind of the Chinese people. That year, I totally fell in love with China.

After returning to Ukraine, my only dream is to be a Chinese teacher to help more people know this particularly interesting, fascinating and unforgettable world of Chinese history, culture and language. After graduating, I started teaching Chinese at Kyiv National Linguistic University. During the lecture, I tried my best to let the students feel the beauty and profundity of Chinese, and encourage them to actively arrange various activities related to Chinese culture and traditional holidays. I hope they can also see China that can be imagined through the stories I have told, although they have not seen it with their own eyes. I not only teach them Chinese, but also convey my love for China to them and let them fall in love with China--the country I love deeply.

In 2003, I got a Chinese Government Scholarship for Ph.D. In all, I have been studying in China for 8 years. During this time, I actively participated in activities organized by the school, performed many times at international student evenings, and liked to travel all over China. In 2008, after graduating from Fudan University with a PhD in Chinese Language and Characters, I also formed my own happy family and became a mother for the first time. In short, in China I have achieved what I dream of and the most important thing in life.

After returning to China, I came to Kyiv National Linguistic University to work and continue to nourish Sinologists and develop Sinology in Ukraine. At the same time, I also became the instructor of the Friendship Association of Confucius Institutes at Kyiv National Linguistic University, actively supporting and participating in various activities of the Confucius Institute, and sometimes bringing children to join. I would make rice dumplings, taste delicious food and experience the Dragon Boat Festival culture with the teachers of the Confucius Institute. In February of this year, at the 2018 New Year Gala themed "Temperature of Culture" jointly organized by the Confucius Institute and the Kyiv Nursing Home, a Chinese teacher Dong Xuesong and I sang the classic song "Red Berry Flower" in Chinese and Russian and send New Year greetings to the elderly. Recently, I have been thinking about how to better develop Sinology in Ukraine, so I actively participate in international cooperation projects. Last year, I returned to China again and was invited to participate in the

"Belt and Road" advanced seminar at Shanghai University. I wanted to have a deeper understanding of the development prospects of Ukrainian Sinology in the "Belt and Road" initiative.

In addition, I have never interrupted my family's contact with China. My three children read many Chinese painting books every day and listen to Chinese stories I told them. My husband and I encourage children to learn Chinese. We send them to the Confucius Institute Children's Chinese Class to learn Chinese every weekend and participate in various activities arranged by the Confucius Institute, which makes them increasingly interested in China. It's worth mentioning that a teacher from the Confucius Institute gave my three sons and daughters Chinese names: Dai Geqiao, Dai Gefei and Dai Gejun. The Chinese word Dai means generation. I hope that our family's fate with China is just like the children's name that can "pass on for many generations".

Generally speaking, my feelings for China can express by the lyrics of the Chinese song I used to sing "Great China": "China, I love you, you will always be in my heart!" From the end of the last century, after listening the story of the Chinese New Year that my mother told me to the present, and into the future, my heart, my spirit and my home will never be separated from China!

做中国与世界沟通交流的桥梁

［埃及］安然

上海外国语大学博士

我的中文名字叫安然，来自埃及开罗。我与中国的缘分始于 2014 年，那年我有幸获得中国政府奖学金就读于山东大学政治学与公共管理学院。经过两年难忘的校园时光和夙兴夜寐的寒窗苦读，我于 2016 年 7 月获得

国际关系专业硕士学位，然后我告别了亲爱的老师、同学和朋友们，依依不舍地离开了校园，登上了返回祖国的飞机。但是我对中国的感情却难以割舍，希望能再回来继续攻读博士学位。“乐而忘返”，2017 年，我申请了孔子学院奖学金，继续我的中国之旅，前往上海外国语大学中东研究所，攻读博士学位。中国历史源远流长，更是一个“文明古国”，知礼明礼是中华民族的传统美德。我曾在开罗大学学习了四年的汉语，自认为对中国的文化历史了如指掌，可是我真的来到中国的时候，才发现自己对中国文化只是略知皮毛，需要再付出千百倍的努力才能真正地了解中国文化。“白驹过隙，岁月荏苒”，生活方式与文化习惯不同所带给我的困惑渐渐烟消云散，我开始融入到了周围的环境中，感受到了中国朋友们的热情与友善，我也努力把自己打造成中国和世界沟通与交流的桥梁。

劝君莫惜金缕衣，劝君惜取少年时

《增广贤文》中有一句话，“一寸光阴一寸金，寸金难买寸光阴”。在中国，我学到了如何去尊重和合理的利用时间，让我生命中的每一分钟都变得有价值，所以我每天管理好我的时间，每天准时起床，在没课的时候，我就去图书馆看书。中国学生很爱学习，深知“黑发不知勤学早，转眼便是白头翁”的道理，图书馆良好的学习氛围深深地影响着我和每一位刻苦读书的同学。我相信，成功终将属于珍惜和懂得合理使用时间的人。

生命不息，运动不止

中国人很喜欢运动。我刚中国的时候，看到了很多中国人特别老年人很喜欢跳广场舞，我曾经和这些老人家交流过，他们说自己这叫“宝刀不老”，这让我很意外。在我们国家，老年人大多都喜静，一般都是坐在电视机前看看肥皂剧，最多是在家里做做家务。中国老年人真的不一样，他们总是充满着活力，将运动玩出很多不同的花样来。而且近年来，越来越多中国年轻人也开始热衷于慢跑等有氧运动了。我以前并不怎么运动，可是到中国之后，只要天气和温度合适，我就会去操场锻炼身体。我现在保持着晨跑的习惯，这让我的健康和精神状态有了很大改善。

读书破万卷，下笔如有神

中国人很喜欢读书，读书让我们收获知识、结识朋友、开阔视野，还能提升思想层次。我现在每周读一本书，“读书破万卷，下笔如有神”，多读书让我产生了许多的写作灵感，更多地了解了中国的文化、历史、思想、政治、经济等各方面的发展现状，让我更上一层楼。“读书之法，在循序而渐进，熟读而精思”，读书也让我学会了如何去思考问题，摆脱愚昧和迷信，我不再是一个空白的人，是书籍赋予了我丰富的知识色彩。

从翻译的角度看中国“走出去”

当下，随着世界对中国的了解越来越多，“汉语热”和“中国热”已然兴起，中国出版的很多作品被翻译成了多国语言，中国走向世界，世界也开始拥抱中国。虽然我的能力有限，但我也尽自己的绵薄之力，将五本中国的优秀书籍翻译成为阿拉伯语。具体书目如下：

时间	书名	作者
2018	《翱翔太空——中国载人航天之路》	唐国东、华强
2017	《从老式车马舟桥到新式交通工具》	董增刚
2017	《从古老发明到高新科技/百年中国社会图谱》	郑国柱
2017—2016	《创造性介入：中国外交的转型》	王逸舟
2015—2016	《解读中国经济》	林毅夫

通过翻译这些作品，我进一步了解了中国的经济、政治、文化、技术发展等情况，比如《解读中国经济》这本书，它以宏大的历史视角展示了中国经济实力两千多年来的跌宕起伏和戏剧性复兴，解读了中国经济增长的源头以及未来增长的前景。这本书的出版得到了所有想要了解中国经济发展的人的关注，我也希望这本书中所提到的经验和教训能够成为所有阿拉伯国家前进道路上的指明灯，帮助我们更好地改革经济。

《创造性介入：中国外交的转型》这本书介绍和探讨的是在变革的大背景下，中国外交的社会基础如何？外交工作怎样适应新的要求？外交转型要走向何方？我们从中也可以提炼出本国外交体制机制反省与改进的所需内容，推动与全球进步时代相适应、相一致的深刻社会转型。

其实，翻译工作有力地推动着世界各国之间的文明互鉴，使其成为各国人民友谊桥梁的根基、推动社会进步的动力以及维护世界和平的纽带。

不入庐山，不识真面目

“读万卷书，行万里路。”放假的时候，我喜欢坐火车去旅游，去感受一下中国的魅力，这是一个现代与古代有机融合的国家。如今，我已经到过很多地方，比如，北京、厦门、深圳、广州、云南、成都、湖南……在火车上，总是有热情的中国人照顾我，与我热情地打招呼，问我“你吃了吗”、“睡得还好吗”。有的时候列车员会专门来看看我，怕我不习惯。在火车上，跟中国人交流是很有意思的，所以通过坐火车我能够了解中国人的性格与习惯。上车时大家互不相识，但是下车时已经成为朋友，怪不得中国诗词中有着“海内存知己，天涯若比邻”、“相知无远近，万里尚为邻”，我真的深有体会。总之，我希望以后能有更多的时间去了解中国的文化、历史、国情和思想等。我相信入了乡随了俗，适应了当地的风土人情，融入这个国家，有朝一日就能成为一名真正的“中国通”。我把自己心的一半留在了埃及，另一半则留给了中国。

习总书记是我的榜样

在中国的多位国家领导中，我很佩服习近平总书记，我觉得他很了不起，我热衷于他的所有演讲，把它们翻译成阿拉伯语。中国人说“谋定而后动，知止而有得”，只有制定正确而适当的政策才能收获成功。我认为习总书记的很多决策非常高瞻远瞩，目标明确，比如“一带一路”倡议贯穿亚欧非大陆，在推动沿线国家发展、解决自身内部产能过剩等问题的同时，更配合构建中日韩三国自由贸易区适度规避东部第一岛链所带来的压力，是十分明智的。这些年来，他一直致力于寻求提升中国国际地位之道，他的一系列促进中国政治和经贸合作发展的外交政策给我留下了深刻的印象，我多么希望阿拉伯国家能有越来越多的领导人发现并学习他身上的闪光点。在他的演讲中，我总能凝练出新的东西，并努力运用到自己的生活当中。

To be a Bridge of Communication and Exchange between China and the World

Hend Sultan Mahmoud Elmahly / Egypt

Shanghai International Studies University, Ph.D. Student

My name is Hend, and my Chinese name is An Ran from Cairo, Egypt. My fate with China began in 2014, when I was lucky to study at the School of Political Science and Public Administration of Shandong University and received a Chinese government scholarship. After two years of unforgettable campus time and assiduous study, I obtained a master's degree in international relations in July 2016, and then I bid farewell to my dear teachers, classmates and friends and left the campus reluctantly. I boarded the plane and returned to the motherland. But my feelings for China always on my mind, and I hope to come back again to continue my study for Ph.D. "Studying in China has much enjoyment and let me forget to return home". In 2017, I applied for a Confucius Institute scholarship to continue my trip to China and went to the Middle East Institute of Shanghai International Studies University to study for a Ph.D degree. China has a long history, and it is also an "ancient civilization." Knowing rituals and being curtesy are the traditional virtues of the Chinese nation. Having studied Chinese at Cairo University for four years, I think I know Chinese culture and history well. When I did come to China, however, I realized that I only knew a little bit about Chinese culture and needed to work thousands of times to truly understand it. "Time passes quickly like a white pony's shadow across a crevice". The confusion brought about by my different lifestyles and cultural habits gradually disappeared. I began to integrate into the surrounding environment and felt the enthusiasm and friendliness of Chinese friends. I also strive to build myself into a bridge of communication and exchange between China and the world.

Love Not Your Golden Dress, I Pray, More than Your Youthful Golden Hours

There is a saying in *The Supplemented Collection of Adages*, "Time is gold, and it is difficult for one to use gold to get time." In China, I learned how to respect and use time reasonably, so that every minute of my life becomes valuable. I manage my time and get up on time every day. When there is no class, I just go to the library for reading. Chinese students love to study, and they know the truth that "When you're young, if you don't cherish the time to study, as time fleets, you'll be regretful as getting old in the blink of an eye." The good learning atmosphere of the library has a profound impact on me and every hard-studying student. I believe that success will ultimately belong to those who cherish and know how to budget time wisely.

Where There is Life, There is Sport

Chinese people like sports very much. When I first arrived in China, I saw a lot of Chinese people, especially elderly people, like square dancing. I once communicated with these elderly people, and they said that they were "old but still vigorous in mind and body", which surprised me. In our country, most elderly people like to be quiet. They usually sit in front of the TV and watch soap operas, at most do housework at home. But the elderly in China are really different. They are always full of vitality and play sports in many different ways. And in recent years, more and more Chinese young people have also become keen on jogging and other aerobic exercises. I didn't do much exercise before, but after arriving in China, as long as the weather and temperature are nice, I will go to the playground to exercise. I now keep the habit of running in the morning, which has greatly improved my health and mentality.

Ample Reading Produces Fluent Writing

Chinese people like reading very much. Reading helps us to gain knowledge, meet friends, broaden our horizons, and improve our thinking. I now read one book a week. "Ample reading produces fluent writing". Reading more has given me a lot of writing inspiration and have more knowledge of Chinese culture, history, thought, politics, economy and so on, which makes me advanced in all respects. "The method of reading is to read in order and step by step, to repeat and to think carefully." Reading has also taught me how to think about problems and get rid of ignorance and superstition. I am no long a person without my own thought. Books have given me a wealth of knowledge.

China's Culture "Going Out" through Translation

At present, as the world learns more about China, the "Chinese fever" and "China fever" have risen. Many works published in China have been translated into multiple languages. China is going to the world, and the world is starting to embrace China. Although my abilities are limited, I also try my best to translate five excellent Chinese books into Arabic. The specific bibliography is as follows:

In 2018, completed the translation work of the book *Soaring into Space-China's Road to Manned Spaceflight* written by Tang Guodong and Hua Qiang;

In 2017, completed the translation work of Dong Zenggang's book *From Old-fashioned Cars, Horses, Boats and Bridges to New Types of Transportation;*

In 2017, completed the translation of Zheng Guozhu's book *From Ancient Inventions to High-tech/A Century of Chinese Social Atlas*;

From 2017 to 2016, completed the translation of Wang Yizhou's book *Creative Intervention: The Transformation of Chinese Diplomacy*;

From 2015 to 2016, completed the translation of Lin Yifu's *Interpretation of Chinese Economy.*

Through the translation of these works, I have a better understanding of China's economic, political, cultural, technological development, etc., such as the book *Interpretation of the Chinese Economy*. It shows the ups and downs and dramatic revival of China's economic power for more than two thousand years from a grand historical perspective and interprets the source of China's economic growth and the prospects for future growth. The publication of this book has attracted the attention of all those who want to understand China's economic development. I also hope that the experience and lessons mentioned in this book can be a guiding light on the way forward for all Arab countries and help us better with economic reform.

The book *Creative Intervention: The Transformation of China's Diplomacy* introduces and discusses these questions: what is the social foundation of China's diplomacy in the context of change? How does diplomatic work adapt to the new requirements? Where is the diplomatic transformation heading? From this, we can also extract the content needed for reflection and improvement of our country's diplomatic system and mechanism, and promote a profound social transformation that is compatible and consistent with the global progressive era.

In fact, translation has effectively promoted mutual learning among civilizations in the world, making it the foundation of a bridge of friendship between peoples of all countries, a driving force for social progress, and a bond for maintaining world peace.

Knowledge Starts with Practice

"Reading thousands of books and traveling thousands of miles", during the holidays, I like to travel by train to feel the charm of China. This is a modern and ancient integration of the country. Nowadays, I have been to many places, such as Beijing, Xiamen, Shenzhen, Guangzhou, Yunnan, Chengdu, Hunan and so on. On the train, there are always enthusiastic Chinese taking care of me and greeting me. They ask me "have you eaten" and "have you slept well?" Sometimes the conductor will come to see me specifically, for fear that I am not used to it. On the train, it is very interesting to communicate with Chinese people, so by chatting with others in the train I can know the Chinese people's characters and habits. When we got on the train, we are strangers, but when we got off the train, we had already become friends. No wonder there are Chinese poems saying that "if you have friends who know your heart, distance cannot keep you apart" and "bosom friends make distance disappear." I really understand it. In short, I hope that I will have more time to understand Chinese culture, history, national conditions and thoughts. I believe that if you do in Rome as Rome does, adapt to the local customs, and integrate into this country, one day you will become a true "China Master". I left half of my heart in Egypt, and the other half in China.

A Fine Model for Me——General Secretary Xi

Among the many national leaders in China, I admire General Secretary Xi Jinping very much. I think he is amazing. I am enthusiastic about all his speeches and translate them into Arabic. The Chinese say that "plan before you move, know when enough is enough and you will gain something." Only by formulating correct and appropriate policies can we achieve success. I think many of General Secretary Xi's decisions are very far-sighted and have clear goals. For example, "The Belt and Road" initiative runs through Asia, Europe and Africa. While promoting the development of countries along the route and solving their own internal overcapacity problems, they also cooperate with the establishment of the free trade areas of China, Japan and Korea. It is very wise for the trade zone to moderately avoid the pressure brought by the first island chain in the east. Over the years, he has been committed to seeking ways to enhance China's international status. His series of foreign policies that promote the development of China's political, economic and trade cooperation have left a deep impression on me. How I hope Arab countries will have more and more leaders discovered and learned the shining points from him. In his speeches, I can always condense new things and try to apply them to my life.

内心对汉语教学的热爱

［俄罗斯］都雅拉
东北联邦大学教师

1992 年的时候，爸爸的朋友送给他一本相册，爸爸对我说这本相册是独一无二的，很难找到。那时候我 7 岁，第一次看到了颜色这么鲜艳的相册。只见封面上画着一个漂亮的女孩，穿着华丽的衣服，她旁边有很多我

不知道的东西，看起来像鸟，也可以说是一种树，非常古怪的树。我特别喜欢那本相册，每次看到封面上的女孩我都会想：她这是在哪里？长得跟我差不多，但是穿的衣服怎么跟我的不一样呢？原来那本相册是中国的，封面上的女孩是中国女孩，她旁边奇怪的鸟和树竟是汉字！那时候我想也不敢想十年以后我会考上大学学习汉语，也知道了那本相册上面的汉字是什么意思。又过了几年，我第一次去中国留学。到中国的第一天就改变了我并影响了我的人生。在中国我去过很多的地方，开阔了眼界，并最终获得了硕士学位，现在我已是大学老师。但每次来到中国仍会想起第一次来中国的情景，回想起那种软软甜甜的感觉。

很多人问我“你为什么当汉语老师？”这个被问及无数次的问题，也困扰了我很多年。是啊，我为什么选择当汉语老师呢？这个问题我不是没想过，但总也找不到答案。真的，工作十多年了，无论面对什么样的问题，我总能说出个一二三来。可这个问题，我竟想不出一点，实在羞愧难当。我内心只是告诉我：“我想当啊”。

就在前几天，我跟我的中国朋友聊天，无意中聊到了这个话题，她没有直接帮我解答我的疑惑，只是说：中国有句话说“真正爱一个人是不需要理由的”。我顿时恍然大悟，原来，我选择教汉语是源于内心的爱，是对一种语言文化的热爱，是对一份职业的热爱，更是对一个国家深深的情结。是这种爱支撑着我，让我可以抵御任何困难、孤独和彷徨。是这种爱，让我斗志昂扬，让我激情满怀。是这种爱，让我奉献了我的青春，实现了我的人生价值。我也常说，我好像在和中国谈恋爱，现在想想，这不是一样的道理吗？

像朋友说的那样，因为是真爱，我当然说不出理由，因为那是内心中的一种感觉，是一种信仰。因为爱而教书育人，使内心中的小爱变成大爱。用佛语说，这是一件功德无量的大事。因此，我既是幸运的，也是幸福的。

My Inner Love to Teaching Chinese Language

Tuiaara Ordakhova / Russia

North-Eastern Federal University, Teacher

In 1992, my father's friend gave him a photo album. He told me that this photo album was unique and difficult to find. At that time, I was 7 years old and I saw such a brightly colored photo album for the first time. I saw a beautiful girl on the cover, wearing gorgeous clothes. There were many things I didn't know beside her. It looked like a bird. It could also be said to be a kind of tree, a very strange tree. I really like that album. Every time I see the girl on the cover, I think: Where is she? She looks similar to me, but how come the clothes she wears are different from mine? It turns out that the album comes from China, the girl on the cover is a Chinese girl, and the strange bird and tree next to her are actually Chinese characters! At that time, I didn't even dare to think that I would go to university to study Chinese in ten years, and know what the Chinese characters in that album meant. A few years later, I went to study in China for the first time. The first day in China changed me and affected my life. I traveled a lot in China, broadened my horizons, and finally got a master's degree. Now I am a university teacher. But every time I come to China, I still think of the first time I came to China, and recall the soft and sweet feeling.

Many people ask me "Why do you choose to be a Chinese teacher?" This question that has been asked countless times has also troubled me for many years. Yes, why did I choose to be a Chinese teacher? I have thought about this question, but I can't find the answer. Well, I have been working for more than ten years, no matter what kind of problem I met with, I can always say something. But to this question, I can't think of any reason, so I am really ashamed. I just follow my heart: "I want to be a Chinese teacher."

Just a few days ago, I chatted with my Chinese friend and came across this topic inadvertently. She didn't directly help me dismiss my confusion. She just said: There is a Chinese saying that "love someone truly does not require a reason." suddenly, the penny dropped and I realized that my choice to teach Chinese stems from my inner love — a love of a language and culture, a love of a profession, and a deep attachment to a country. It is this kind of love that encourages me and pushes me to resist any difficulties, loneliness and hesitation. It is this kind of love that makes me motivated and full of passion. It is this kind of love that urges me to dedicate my youth and realize the value of my life. I also often say that I seem to be in a relationship with China. Thinking about it now, isn't this the same truth?

Like my friend said, because it is true love, I certainly can't give a reason, because it is a feeling in my heart, it is a kind of faith. Teaching and educating people because of love, turning the little love in the heart into a big love. In Buddhist language, this is a great event of immense merit. Therefore, I am both lucky and happy.

汉语是打开世界大门的钥匙

[阿富汗]哈密
喀布尔大学孔子学院讲师

拿到语言的钥匙

2010年3月高考成绩出来后，我就急急忙忙地跑去网吧查看我的成绩。输入准考证号后，我看到我考上了喀布尔大学，但是并没有被喜欢的

专业录取，而是被调剂到喀布尔大学孔子学院中文系。当时我回到家已经是傍晚，家里还停电了，我感到非常失望，不知不觉就哭了。第二天我想去学校听听班主任的建议，当时老师就对我说："别看现在社会上你们专业没有其他专业受欢迎，但你们的专业是一把钥匙，一把进入社会的钥匙。"老师还帮我分析了我的专业前景，"随着中国经济迅速地发展，懂中国语言的人才也随之会有更大的发展空间。这就是语言带给你的神奇魔力。"老师的这一席话让我醍醐灌顶，下定决心去读这个专业。无论是将来进入社会，还是发展自己，我都需要这把钥匙。

打开世界的大门

从那时候开始，我就慢慢对中国的语言和文化产生了兴趣。2012 年，我第一次离开家人，第一次离开阿富汗来到中国山西太原，第一次体验到跨文化的生活……许许多多的第一次美好时刻和体验都成为我人生中忘不掉的记忆。

2014 年底，我以优异的成绩从喀布尔大学孔子学院（中文系）毕业，并通过面试和试讲，正式成为喀布尔大学中文系的本土汉语教师。在教学过程中，我认真备课，积极组织课堂教学，想尽一切办法激发阿富汗学生学习汉语的兴趣，提高阿富汗学生学习汉语的积极性。同时，我也深刻地体会到，要想成为一名合格的汉语教师，我不仅需要具备语言能力，还需要了解中国文化与社会，漫漫长路我仍需要继续努力前行。

2015 年是阿富汗和中国建交 60 周年，也是"中阿友好合作年"，对我来说这也是非常难忘的一年。我作为喀布尔大学孔子学院中文系的一员，有幸参加了一系列重大纪念活动，见证了这一重要的历史时刻。2015 年 1 月 20 日，在庆祝中阿建交 60 周年的纪念仪式上，我代表阿富汗用汉语进行了发言。我有幸见到了中国国家领导人和我们国家的总统，并与他们握

手交谈。我人生中第一次深刻地感受到，学习中文，学好一门语言，会对一个人的人生产生如此重大的影响。因此，未来我希望自己能成为中阿友谊的使者，为两国交往贡献自己的一分力量。

拥有第二个家

经过阿富汗两年的汉语教学，我体会到要想进一步提高阿富汗的汉语教学层次，我还需要继续进修汉语，加强自身的专业知识。2016年，我申请到了孔子学院奖学金和南亚汉语师资办项目的硕士专业，并被华东师范大学录取。在华东师范大学的两年学习生活中，我不仅认真地参与了专业知识的课堂学习，还参加了一些课外活动，如参加衢州的祭孔大典、国际文化节表演话剧《蔡文姬》等活动，并在“我的‘一带一路’”全球中文演讲大赛中获得三等奖。这些活动都让我受益匪浅。

我虽然不是中国人，但是一直关注中国各方面的事情。不管是新闻、运动还是电影，只要跟中国有关系我都会看。看中国运动比赛的时候，我也像中国人一样给中国队加油助威。我是阿富汗人，但是中国也是我第二个家。汉语这把神奇的钥匙，为我打开了一个新的大门，让我看到悠久灿烂的历史、热情友善的人民、自强不息的精神。

继续传递钥匙

阿富汗和中国历来就是友好邻邦，随着中国“一带一路”计划的实施，两国之间将会开展并加强各个层面的交流与合作。因此，阿富汗需要更多的汉语和翻译人才。作为一名阿富汗本土汉语教师，我希望编写适合阿富汗汉语教学的教材，成为更加称职的汉语教师，将“汉语”这把神奇的钥匙传递给更多阿富汗人民，为两国之间的友谊和发展做出贡献。

Chinese Language, the Key to Open the Door to the World

Hamid Gholami / Afghanistan

Confucius Institute of Kabul University, Lecturer

Get the Key to Language

After the college entrance examination results came out in March 2010, I hurried to the Internet cafe to check my results. After entering the admission ticket number, I saw that I was admitted to Kabul University, but I was not admitted to my favorite major. Instead, I was transferred to the Chinese Department of the Confucius Institute at Kabul University. It was early evening when I got home, and there was a power outage at home. I was very disappointed and cried without knowing it. The next day I wanted to go to school and listen to the advice of the class teacher. At that time, the teacher said to me: "Don't think your major is not as popular as other majors in society, but your major is a key, a key to entering society." The teacher also helped me analyze my professional prospects, "With the rapid development of China's economy, talents who understand Chinese language will also have more room for development. This is the magical power that language brings to you." This remark gave me an initiation and made up my mind to study this major. I need this key whether I enter society in the future or develop my own ability and strength.

Open the Door to the World

Since then, I have slowly developed an interest in Chinese language and culture. In 2012, I left my family for the first time, left Afghanistan for the first time and came to Taiyuan, Shanxi, China, and experienced the life of intercultural communication for the first time...Many of the first beautiful moments and experiences have become unforgettable Memory.

At the end of 2014, I graduated from the Confucius Institute (Chinese Department) of Kabul University with excellent grades, and through interviews and trial lectures, I officially became a local Chinese teacher in the Chinese Department of Kabul University. During the teaching process, I carefully prepared lessons, actively organized classroom teaching, and tried every means to stimulate the interest of Afghan students in learning Chinese, and improve the enthusiasm of Afghan students in learning Chinese. At the same time, I also deeply realized that in order to become a qualified Chinese teacher, I not only need to have language skills, but also need to understand Chinese culture and society. I still need to continue working hard for a long way.

2015 marks the 60th anniversary of the establishment of diplomatic relations between Afghanistan and China, and it is also the "China-Arab Friendship and Cooperation Year". It is also a very unforgettable year for me. As a member of the Chinese Department of the Confucius Institute at Kabul University, I have the honor to participate in a series of major commemorative activities and witness this important historical moment. On January 20, 2015, at the commemorative ceremony celebrating the 60th anniversary of the establishment of diplomatic relations between China and Afghanistan, I spoke in Chinese on behalf of Afghanistan. I was fortunate enough to meet the leaders of China and the president of our country, and shook hands with them. For the first time in my life, I deeply felt that learning Chinese and a good language can have such a significant impact on a person's life. Therefore, in the future, I hope that I can become an envoy of China-Arab friendship and contribute my own strength to the exchanges between the two countries.

The Second Hometown

After two years of teaching Chinese in Afghanistan, I realized that if I want to further improve the level of Chinese teaching in Afghanistan, I still need to continue to study Chinese and strengthen my professional knowledge. In 2016, I applied for the Confucius Institute Scholarship and the Master's degree in the South Asian Chinese Teachers Office Program, and was admitted to East China Normal University. During the two years of study and life in East China Normal University, I not only seriously participated in the classroom learning of professional knowledge, but also participated in some extracurricular activities, such as participating in the Confucian Memorial Ceremony in Quzhou, performing the drama "Cai Wenji" at the International Cultural Festival and other activities. I also won the third prize in the My "Belt and Road" global Chinese speech contest. These activities have benefited me a lot.

Although I am not Chinese, I have always been concerned about all aspects of China. Whether it is news, sports or movies, I will watch as long as it has something to do with China. When watching Chinese sports games, I also cheer for the Chinese team like a Chinese. I am an Afghan, but China is also my second home. The magical key of Chinese has opened a new door for me, allowing me to see a long and splendid history, a warm and friendly people, and a spirit of self-improvement.

Continue to Pass the Key

Afghanistan and China have always been friendly neighbors. With the implementation of China's "Belt and Road" initiative, the two countries will develop and strengthen exchanges and cooperation at all levels. Therefore, Afghanistan needs more Chinese and translators. As a native Afghan Chinese teacher, I hope to compile textbooks suitable for Afghan Chinese teaching, to become a more competent Chinese teacher, pass the magic key of "Chinese" to more Afghan people, and contribute to the friendship and development between the two countries.

从杂技到文化

［埃及］丽丽
埃及军队语言学院中文讲师

我的中国故事始于30年前，当时我是个五六岁的孩子。每到周末上午，埃及电视台有个儿童节目叫“儿童世界”。这个节目最有意思的部分是中国杂技团的表演，演员有小孩也有青年。节目独特而精彩，我时常被打动。直到现在，“抖空竹”表演还清晰地存在于我的记忆之中。那时，我问了爸爸一个问题：“中国在哪里？我想去那儿学习杂技。”爸爸笑着说：“你一定会去的。”

没想到10年后，我考上了埃及艾因夏姆斯大学语言学院中文系。我虽然没学杂技，但是学了汉语和中国文化，这已经让我感到十分满足。学习汉语时，我遇到了很多困难，但是我总是记得我妈妈20年前对我说的话：“中国是未来，你要认真学习未来的语言。”于是我刻苦学习、加倍努力，4年持之以恒的学习给了我很多机会了解中国文化、社会历史和民间习俗。毕业后，我成为一名翻译，在与中国人沟通的过程中又更加深入地了解了这一古老的民族，这个拥有和埃及一样悠久历史的国家。

2013年中国政府提出了“一带一路”倡议，坚持共商、共建、共享的原则，努力实现沿线区域基础设施更加完善，更加安全高效，以形成更高水平的陆海空交流网络。同时使投资贸易的便利化水平更有效的提升，建立高品质、高标准的自由贸易区域网，使沿线各国经济联系更加紧密，政治互信更加深入，人文交流更加广泛。

中国文化在埃及社会的影响力很大。通过中埃两国政府不断的合作，普通的埃及老百姓能够看到丰富多彩的中国艺术演出，可以上汉语班和武术班，欣赏中国电影，聆听有关中国社会情况的讲座。学习中国文化显然已经成为埃及社会的一股潮流。

2016年，我有幸参加了中埃文化年的筹办工作，通过自己的翻译工作为两国文化交流做出了贡献。同年，我也有机会参加了北京师范大学中国文化培训班。爬长城、看故宫、吃烤鸭、游览北京故宫博物院和颐和园，我真真切切地体验了地道的中国社会生活。

前不久，我和我的同事们共同努力，成功举办了首届中国阿拉伯国家文学论坛。一百多位中阿知名作家、文学家和翻译家齐聚一堂，互相交流，让我受益匪浅。

我的中国故事还在继续着，我期待每天都能获得新的体验。

From Acrobatics to Culture

Reham Gamal Mohamed / Egypt

Egyptian Army Language Academy, Chinese Lecturer

My Chinese story began 30 years ago, when I was a five or six year old child. Every weekend morning, the Egyptian TV station has a children's program called "Children's World". The most interesting part of this show is the performance of the Chinese Acrobatic Troupe. The actors have children and young people. The show is unique and exciting, and I am often moved. Until now, the performance of "Diabolo Shaking" still clearly exists in my memory. At that time, I asked my father a question: "Where is China? I want to go there to learn acrobatics." Dad smiled and said, "You will definitely go."

Unexpectedly, 10 years later, I was admitted to the Chinese Department of Language School of Ain Shams University in Egypt. Although I didn't learn acrobatics, but I learned Chinese and Chinese culture, which made me feel very satisfied. When learning Chinese, I encountered many difficulties, but I always remember what my mother said to me 20 years ago, "China is the future, you should study the language of the future seriously." So I study hard and work harder. Four years of persistent study gave me many opportunities to learn about Chinese culture, social history and folk customs. After graduating, I became a translator, and in the process of communicating with the Chinese, I learned more about this ancient nation, a country with the same long history as Egypt.

In 2013, the Chinese government proposed the "Belt and Road" initiative, adhering to the principles of extensive consultation, joint construction, and sharing, and strive to achieve a more complete, safer and more efficient regional infrastructure along the route to form a higher level of land, sea and air exchanges. At the same time, the facilitation level of investment and trade will be more effectively improved, and a high-quality, high-standard free trade area network will be established, so that countries along the route will have closer economic ties, deeper political mutual trust, and more extensive cultural exchanges.

Chinese culture has a great influence in Egyptian society. Through the continuous cooperation between the governments of China and Egypt, ordinary Egyptians can see a variety of Chinese art performances, go to Chinese classes and martial arts classes, enjoy Chinese movies, and listen to lectures on Chinese social conditions. Learning Chinese culture has obviously become a trend in Egyptian society. In 2016, I was fortunate to participate in the preparation of the China-Egypt Cultural Year and contributed to the cultural exchanges between the two countries through my own translation work. In the same year, I also had the opportunity to participate in a Chinese culture training class at Beijing Normal University. Climbing the Great Wall, seeing the Forbidden City, eating roast duck, visiting the Palace Museum and the Summer Palace in Beijing, I really experienced the authentic Chinese social life. Not long ago, my colleagues and I worked together to successfully host the first China Arab Literature Forum. More than one hundred well-known Chinese and Arab writers, writers and translators gathered together to communicate with each other, which benefited me a lot. My Chinese story continues, and I look forward to having new experiences every day.

薪火相传

［俄罗斯］奥莉亚

俄罗斯科学院远东分院历史学民族学研究所助理

我第一次认识中国是在二十世纪末。这么多年来，我和它相隔甚远，爸爸就成了我们之间的纽带。我经常看到爸爸看中文书、翻译中文，但我没有想到有一天会和他一样。我一直都想看看这个世界，当然，也很想了

解中国。它离我是那么的遥远，却也近在咫尺。

我出生在符拉迪沃斯托克。1991 年，这个封闭的港口正式对外国人开放。中国商人开始来到这个城市，随之出现了一些大的中国市场，这也成了边境城市符拉迪沃斯托克的特色之一。

我在大学开始学习中文，但我却没有机会去中国。大学毕业后，我进入俄罗斯科学院远东分院的历史研究所汉学研究中心攻读博士学位。该中心主要研究中国东北问题，我的研究方向是文化。我写过一篇关于中国东北文化的论文，题目是“中国东北文化改革与发展（1978—2008）”。

我第一次来中国是在 2008 年。我来到了哈尔滨，在黑龙江大学学习了三个月的中文。后来由于工作关系，我去过长春和沈阳。此外，我还去过著名的旅游城市如北京、大连、三亚、秦皇岛、亚布力以及边境口岸黑河和绥芬河。当地居民的淳朴善良，尤其是年轻人，给我留下了深刻的印象。我在公交车上经常能看到青年男女给老年人让座，这令我十分难忘。

在社会科学界，对同样的问题有不同的看法。我读过一位社会科学家的评论，他认为俄罗斯人民和中国人民之间存在着难以逾越的文化鸿沟。但是在我看来，我们两国人民之间并不存在这种鸿沟，存在的是一座宏伟，宽阔，坚实的桥梁。2016 年有一次我带 5 岁的儿子去一位中国朋友家做客。她有一个 13 岁的女儿，比我儿子大一些。尽管两个孩子年龄有差异还有不同的文化背景，但他们却有着共同的“语言”。他们通过画各种图画来交流，虽然彼此语言不通却能够了解对方说什么，玩得非常愉快。这恰恰就是友谊与相互理解的典型实例。从那之后我的孩子最大的愿望就是去中国。因此我想，我和中国的渊源可能会一直延续下去。

From Generation to Generation

Olga Risukhina / Russia

Institute of History and Ethnography, Far Eastern Branch, Russian Academy of Sciences, Assistant

I first met China at the end of the 20th century. Over the years, I have been so far apart from it, and Dad has become the bond between us. I often see my father reading Chinese documents and translating Chinese, but I did not expect to be like him one day. I have always wanted to see the world, of course, I also want to understand China. It is so far away from me, but also close at hand.

I was born in Vladivostok. In 1991, this closed port was officially opened to foreigners. Chinese businessmen began to come to this city, and some large Chinese markets appeared, which became one of the characteristics of the border city of Vladivostok.

I started to learn Chinese in university, but I didn't have the opportunity to go to China. After graduating from university, I entered the Sinology Research Center of the History Institute of the Far East Branch of the Russian Academy of Sciences to study for a PhD. The center mainly studies Northeast China issues, and my research direction is culture. I wrote an essay on the culture of Northeast China, the title is "The Reform and Development of Northeast China Culture (1978-2008)".

I first came to China in 2008. I came to Harbin and studied Chinese at Heilongjiang University for three months. Later, due to work, I went to Changchun and Shenyang. In addition, I have also been to famous tourist cities such as Beijing, Dalian, Sanya, Qinhuangdao, Yabuli, as well as border ports Heihe and Suifenhe. The honesty and kindness of the local people, especially the young people, left a deep impression on me. I often see young men and women giving seats to the elderly on the bus, which is very unforgettable for me.

In the social sciences, there are different views on different issues. I have read a comment from a social scientist who believes that there is an insurmountable cultural gap between the Russian people and the Chinese people. But in my opinion, there is no such gap between our two peoples, but a magnificent, wide, and solid bridge. In 2016, once I took my 5-year-old son to a Chinese friend's house. She has a 13-year-old daughter who is older than my son. Although the two children have different ages and different cultural backgrounds, they share a “common language”. They communicated by drawing various pictures. Although they could not understand each other's language, they were able to understand what each other said and had a great time. This is just a typical example of friendship and mutual understanding. Since then, my son’s biggest wish is to go to China. So I think my relationship with China may continue.

汉学家的“中国结”|我的中国梦

［格鲁吉亚］玛莉雅
华鑫建筑有限公司翻译

我叫玛莉雅，是格鲁吉亚人。格鲁吉亚位于高加索地区的黑海沿岸，北邻俄罗斯，南接土耳其、亚美尼亚、阿塞拜疆。格鲁吉亚虽与中国相隔万里，但早在西汉丝绸之路开通时，两国就已有来往。自 1991 年格鲁吉亚独立，两国便正式建交。如今，两国的友谊正不断加深。格鲁吉亚人民一直很尊重中国并且很喜欢中国的传统文化。自西汉丝绸之路开通后，中国的文化在格鲁吉亚便大受欢迎。在格鲁吉亚，我们每年，有时甚至一年会举办多次中国文化作品展览会。最近几年，格鲁尼亚学汉语的学生越来越多，他们与我一样，都有个“中国梦。”随着经济全球化，古时“千里之隔”的两国如今越来越近，人们的“心距”也越来越近。真心希望我美丽的国家与我的第二故乡——中国越来越好。

我对中国很感兴趣，这兴趣的小火苗还要从我小时候开始说起。我的国家每年都会举办中国文化展览会，每次展览会都必定少不了我。每次去看展览会，我都会看到很多新奇有趣的东西。除此之外，我还看中国电影、听与中国有关的所有节目。慢慢地，我对这位大国的兴趣越来越浓厚。

2003年，我做出了一个对我的一生都至关重要的决定：学习汉语。一开始很多朋友和亲戚怀疑我的决定，他们说汉语非常难，学习汉语会十分辛苦。他们一直问我为什么做出这样一个决定？到现在我一直都有这样一个相同的答案：如果你能给我介绍一个比中国有意思和比中国热情的国家，我就改变主意。汉语与格鲁吉亚的语言分属两种语系，因此，在学习汉语过程中我遇到了很多挫折，但什么都阻挡不了我想学习汉语的心，最终，我终于坚持了下来并且学会了汉语，这为我留学中国打下了坚实的基础。

终于，2007年，20岁的我实现了我的梦想来到了中国。在中国留学的岁月里，第一年是最难忘的。我永远都不会忘记武汉华中师范大学留给我的记忆，在我眼中，中国永远是我第二故乡。在中国，我不仅学会了中国的语言了解了中国的文化，我更学会了生活。2009年我获得了国家奖学金并且在中国攻读硕士学位，这三年是我一生中最难忘的时光。在这三年里，我成长了很多。格鲁吉亚是个很小的国家，它的总面积为69700平方米，并且人口不到4000000人。在这么小的国家生活的人第一次去世界上最大的国家之一生活对我来说是一种挑战。中国浩繁的人口、拥堵的交通、飞快的生活速度对那时候的我来说很难习惯。但在中国朋友的帮助和支持下，我很快习惯了中国的生活节奏。我依稀记得第一天上课时，老师让我们外国学生介绍自己的国家。我一提到格鲁吉亚，中国同学和老师就问：格鲁吉亚是不是斯大林的故乡？格鲁吉亚是不是苏联的国家？格鲁吉亚是不是俄罗斯的邻居？我当时觉得很奇怪：世界上竟有这么多人不知道格鲁吉亚的位置，不了解格鲁吉亚的历史。但同时我心里也感觉很自豪：世界上最大的国家之一已经开始认识格鲁吉亚，那我们国家的前途便是光明的！

我永远不会忘记中国同学对我的支持和帮助。他们尽最大的努力帮助我了解中国。放假时我们经常一起出去旅游，他们还教我中国历史、书法、歌曲和舞蹈等。我们还一起过中国的传统节日，尝了中国的特色食物。这样我对中国的认识慢慢变得丰富了，而我对中国的兴趣也更加浓厚了。我回国之后很多人问我："中国人天天光吃米饭吗？用筷子难不难？"我听到这些问题时心里觉得很可笑，因为他们很多人不知道中国的菜其实非常丰富，也不知道用筷子甚至比用刀叉还方便。回格鲁吉亚之后我的中国同学也经常来格鲁吉亚旅游，他们都很喜欢格鲁吉亚。他们说虽然格鲁吉亚面积小，人口少，但是格鲁吉亚非常漂亮，就像一个小天堂。

学习汉语改变了我的人生，并且给我打开很多扇门。2012 年硕士学习生涯结束了，我告别了中国回到了格鲁吉亚。从 2012 年起，格鲁吉亚开始积极地投入国际社会，国家经济也慢慢地发展起来，因此，格鲁吉亚逐渐受到了国际社会的关注。中国与格鲁吉亚的关系也越来越密切，两国政府代表互访也越来越频繁。对于我的国家来说，最重要的是中国对于格鲁吉亚领土的完整和主权独有的支持。

我回国之后有点紧张，因为一切都得从零开始，但是我突然发现会说汉语的人更容易成功。回国后，我在一家中国公司工作，同时在一家学校教汉语，希望给年轻的学生一个机会，让他们更加了解中国。但是我最大的目的和愿望是：为中国和格鲁吉亚的关系做出贡献，通过我的经验和知识加深两国之间的友谊。对格鲁吉亚来说，中国是个大哥并且一直在帮助它。因为我的国家朋友不多，所以中国对格鲁尼亚的支持都是无价的。

我相信未来中国与格鲁吉亚的友谊会更加深厚，并且两国会永远互相支持和永远互相合作。

My Chinese Dream

Mariam Okromtchedlishvili / Georgia
Huaxin Construction Company Limited, Translator

My name is Mariam and I am from Georgia. Georgia is located on the Black Sea coast in the Caucasus region, bordered by Russia in the north and Turkey, Armenia and Azerbaijan in the south. Although Georgia is separated from China by tens of thousands of miles, the two countries have communicated since the opening of the Silk Road in the Western Han Dynasty. Since Georgia's independence in 1991, the two countries have officially established diplomatic relations. Today, the friendship between the two countries is constantly deepening. The Georgian people have always respected China and loved Chinese traditional culture. Since the opening of the Silk Road in the Western Han Dynasty, Chinese culture has become very popular in Georgia. In Georgia, we hold several exhibitions of Chinese cultural works every year, sometimes even a year. In recent years, there have been more and more students studying Chinese in Grünia. Like me, they all have a "Chinese dream." With economic globalization, the two countries that were "thousand miles apart" in ancient times are now getting closer and closer. People's "heart distance" is getting shortened. I sincerely hope that my beautiful country and my second hometown — China are getting better and better.

I am very interested in China, and the small flames of this interest started when I was young. My country holds a Chinese cultural exhibition every year, and every exhibition must have me. Every time I go to an exhibition, I see a lot of novel and interesting things. In addition, I also watch Chinese movies and listen to all programs related to China. Slowly, I became more and more interested in this big country.

In 2003, I made a decision that was crucial to my life: to learn Chinese. At first, many friends and relatives doubted my decision. They spoke Chinese very hard, and learning Chinese would be very hard. They keep asking me why I made such a decision? I have always had the same answer until now: If you can introduce me to a country that is more interesting and enthusiastic than China, I will change my mind. Chinese and Georgian languages belong to two language families. Therefore, I encountered a lot of setbacks in the process of learning Chinese, but nothing can stop me from wanting to learn Chinese. In the end, I finally persevered and learned Chinese. I have laid a solid foundation for studying in China.

Finally, in 2007, at the age of 20, I realized my dream and came to China. In the years of studying in China, the first year is the most memorable. I will never forget the memory left to me by Wuhan Huazhong Normal University. In my eyes, China will always be my second hometown. In China, I not only learned the Chinese language and the Chinese culture, I also learned to live. In 2009, I won a national scholarship and studied for a master's degree in China. These three years are the most memorable time in my life. In these three years, I have grown a lot. Georgia is a very small country with a total area of 69,700 square meters and a population of less than 4,000,000. It is a challenge for me to live in one of the largest countries in the world for people living in such a small country. China's huge population, congested traffic, and fast life speed were difficult for me at that time. But with the help and support of Chinese friends, I quickly got used to the pace of life in China. I vaguely remember that on the first day of class, the teacher asked us foreign students to introduce our country. When I mentioned Georgia, Chinese classmates and teachers asked: Is Georgia the hometown of Stalin? Is Georgia a country of the former Soviet Union? Is Georgia a neighbor of Russia? I thought it was strange at the time: there are so many people in the world who don't know the location of Georgia and don't understand the history of Georgia. But at the same time, I also feel very proud in my heart: one of the largest countries in the world has begun to know Georgia, so the future of our country is bright!

I will never forget the support and help from Chinese classmates. They did their best to help me understand China. During holidays, we often travel together. They also taught me Chinese history, calligraphy, songs and dances. We also spent traditional Chinese festivals together and tasted Chinese special food. In this way, my knowledge of China has gradually become richer, and my interest in China has also become stronger. After I returned to China, many people asked me: "Do Chinese people eat rice every day? Is it difficult to use chopsticks?" When I heard these questions, I thought it was ridiculous, because many of them didn't know that Chinese cuisine was actually very rich. Know that using chopsticks is even more convenient than using a knife and fork. After returning to Georgia, my Chinese classmates also often travel to Georgia. They all like Georgia. They said that although Georgia is small and has a small population, Georgia is very beautiful, like a little paradise.

Learning Chinese has changed my life and opened many doors for me. The master's study career in 2012 is over, and I bid farewell to China and returned to Georgia. Since 2012, Georgia began to actively participate in the international community, and the national economy has gradually developed. Therefore, Georgia has gradually received the attention of the international community. The relationship between China and Georgia is getting closer, and the exchange of visits between government representatives of the two countries has become more frequent. For my country, the most important thing is China's unique support for the territorial integrity and sovereignty of Georgia.

I was a little nervous after returning home, because everything had to start from scratch, but I suddenly found that people who can speak Chinese are more likely to succeed. After returning to China, I worked in a Chinese company and taught Chinese at a school at the same time. I hope to give young students a chance to learn more about China. But my biggest goal and wish is to contribute to the relationship between China and Georgia, and to deepen the friendship between the two countries through my experience and knowledge. For Georgia, China is a big brother and has been helping it. Because I don't have many friends in my country, China's support for Georgia is priceless.

I believe that the friendship between China and Georgia will be deeper in the future, and the two countries will always support and cooperate with each other.

汉学家的“中国结”|我的中国记忆

［突尼斯］瓦利德
人民日报社、人民网外籍专家

我是瓦利德，今年33岁了，来自突尼斯。我在中国生活已经有10年。2007年，我从突尼斯高等语言学院中文系本科毕业。2008年到2017年，我又分别在北京语言大学和北京大学攻读了硕士和博士。

我跟中国很有缘分。在我小的时候，对中国的了解比较少，只听说过长城、黄河，还了解中国的人口数量是世界上最多的等简单的知识。

90 年代初，在改革开放政策的推动下，中国对外贸易范围进一步扩大，越来越多的中国元素走进突尼斯。当时，我们能够接触一些中国产品，但都是比较低端的，比如电池、锁具、纺针、鞋油等，而这些产品包装上都有不少的汉字。

汉字这一最具独特性的文字，引起了我的注意，激发了我的好奇心。每次，我都会找到那些中国产品的包装，并且将上面的汉字抄下来。不过因为刚刚接触这一神奇的符号，每次都是随意写画，自己并不能明白其中的含义。至今，我印象最深刻的是“中国制造”这四个字，因为这四个字我能理解其中的含义，而且配有英文法文或阿拉伯文的翻译，如英文“made in china”。另外，中国两个字的笔画简单，所以对我来说比较好写，不是很复杂。20 世纪 90 年代初全突尼斯都没有中文课，有时候会想如果那个时候开设汉语课该多好，我一定会投入极大的兴趣去学习汉语。长大以后，到了初中和高中的阶段，我似乎对汉字没有那么大的兴趣了。一方面因为没有语言环境，另一方面随着中国的产品越来越多，大街小巷都是中文的说明，慢慢地，我已经习惯了这个原本陌生的文字，兴趣就减弱了。但同时，我对中国的兴趣开始转移到其他方面。慢慢地，随着 90 年代中国经济的飞速发展，关于中国的信息越来越多，突尼斯人对中国的认识也越来越丰富了。通过媒体，我能了解到关于中国的各种说法，例如中国奇迹、黄色巨人、睡醒之龙等。

我所就读的高中，是分不同专业的。我读的是经济管理专业，专业的敏感度让我更关注中国。高考结束以后，在填写志愿时，我先把第一选项留空，然后把第 2—10 选项都填写上经济方面的专业。当时我心里有一个大胆的想法，第一志愿我想选中文专业，但心里有点忐忑，因为当时学习中文的人是很少的，而且读了别的专业大概能知道毕业了以后做什么工作，但学中文就不可知了。在我犹豫不决时，我的一个哥哥，他非常鼓励我学习中文，并且说中国经济越来越好了，毕业后肯定不发愁找到好工作。犹豫了几天后，我最终下定决心学习中文！

从突尼斯到中国，从突尼斯高等语言学院到北京语言大学，再到北京大学，从几千字的本科毕业论文，到几万字的硕士论文，再到十几万字的博士论文，我的中文和我一同成长着。在此期间，我认识到中文不单是一个专业，同时也是我了解中国文化、步入中国社会的桥梁。

最终，我从刚开始一个对中国感到好奇的 20 多岁年轻人慢慢变成了一个融入中国社会的“老人”。是中国让我认真思考故乡的意义。后来我意识到真正的故乡在人的记忆里，在哪里生活、认识什么样的人，走到了哪座城市市哪条街，经历了哪些愉快的和不愉快的，都会深刻地保存在记忆里。而这些记忆会跟你所生活的地方密切地联系在一起。当你想

离开这个地方的时候，会发现实际上你已经属于这儿了。离开就成为人与自身记忆的一种撕裂。对我来说，我在中国生活了 10 年，虽然我不属于中国，但感觉中国属于我，中国已经变成我关于故乡记忆的一个重要组成部分。现在，我认为我有两个故乡，一个是我的祖国突尼斯，另一个就是中国。

My Chinese Memory

Walidabdallah / Tunisia

People's Daily-people.cn, Foreign expert

I am Walid and I am 33 years old and I am from Tunisia. I have lived in China for 10 years. In 2007, I graduated with a bachelor's degree from the Chinese Department of the Higher School of Languages in Tunisia. From 2008 to 2017, I went to Beijing Language and Culture University and Peking University to study for master's and doctoral degrees respectively. I have a lot of fate with China. When I was young, I knew little about China. I only heard about the simple knowledge that the Great Wall, the Yellow River and the population of China are the largest in the world. In the early 1990s, under the promotion of the reform and opening policy, China's foreign trade scope was further expanded, and more and more Chinese elements entered Tunisia. At that time, we were able to access some Chinese products, but they were relatively low-end, such as batteries, locks, spinning needles, shoe polish, etc., and there were many Chinese characters on the packaging of these products.

Chinese characters, the most unique text, caught my attention and aroused my curiosity. Every time, I found the packaging of those Chinese products and copied down the Chinese characters. But because I just came into contact with this magical symbol, I always write and write randomly, and I can't understand the meaning. So far, I am most impressed by the four words "Made in China", because I can understand the meaning of these four words, and they have English French or Arabic translations, such as English "made in china". In addition, the strokes of the two Chinese characters are simple, so it is easier for me to write, not very complicated. In the early 1990s, there were no Chinese classes in Tunisia. Sometimes I wondered if Chinese classes were offered at that time. I would definitely devote great interest to learning Chinese. When I grew up, I was in the middle and high school stages, and I didn't seem to be so interested in Chinese characters anymore. On the one hand, because there is no language environment, on the other hand, as there are more and more Chinese products, the streets and alleys are all explained in Chinese. Gradually, I have become accustomed to this unfamiliar text, and my interest has diminished. But at the same time, my interest in China began to shift to other areas. Slowly, with the rapid development of China's economy in the 1990s, there is more and more information about China, and the Tunisian people's understanding of China has become more and more abundant. Through the media, I can learn about various theories about China, such as the Chinese miracle, the yellow giant, and the waking dragon.

The high school I attended was divided into different majors. I am studying economics and management, and my awareness of economics makes me pay more attention to China. After the college entrance examination is over, when filling in the volunteers, I leave the first option blank, and then fill in the second to tenth options with majors in economics. At that time, I had a bold idea. On my first choice, I wanted to choose Chinese as a major, but I was a little nervous, because there were very few people studying Chinese at the time, and after studying other majors, I probably knew what to do after graduation. But learning Chinese is unknowable. When I was hesitant, one of my brothers encouraged me to learn Chinese and said that China's economy is getting better and better. After graduation, he will definitely not worry about finding a good job. After a few days of hesitation, I finally made up my mind to learn Chinese!

From Tunisia to China, from Tunisia Advanced Language Institute to Beijing Language and Culture University, to Peking University, from undergraduate thesis with a few thousand words, to master thesis with tens of thousands of words, to doctoral thesis with 100,000 words, my Chinese Grow with me. During this period, I realized that Chinese is not only a major, but also a bridge for me to understand Chinese culture and step into Chinese society. In the end, from the beginning, a young man in his 20s who was curious about China became an “old man” who was integrated into Chinese society. It was China that made me think seriously about the meaning of my hometown. Later I realized that my real hometown is in people’s memory, where I live, what kind of people I know, which city or street I went to, and the pleasant and unpleasant experiences I experienced will be deeply preserved in memory. And these memories will be closely linked to the place where you live. When you want to leave this place, you will find that you actually belong here. Leaving becomes a kind of tear between the memory of man and himself. For me, I have lived in China for 10 years. Although I do not belong to China, I feel that China belongs to me. China has become an important part of my hometown memories. Now, I think I have two hometowns, one is my home country Tunisia, the other is China.

汉学家的“中国结”｜一笔一画汉字缘，一带一路中国梦

［乌克兰］曾子儒

同济大学国际文化交流学院硕士研究生

我和中国的故事就像汉字一样，都由一笔一画勾勒而成，在学习汉语、走向中国的道路上，我时刻不能忘记是如何一步一步地由过去走到今天的。

7 岁生日那天，家人送给我一本儿童地图册作为礼物。那是我第一次在地图上发现这个神秘的国度——中国。从此，小小的内心诞生了一个大大的梦想——我要学习她的语言，了解她的历史文化，继续去探究她的神秘。地图册不知被我翻了多少次，它旧了，破了，但直到今天我还一直珍藏着它，因为它是我学习汉语、走向中国的“领路人”。

时间过得真快，转眼来到高中毕业面临我人生中第一个重要的选择的时刻。是的，我没有放弃埋藏在心里十年的梦想。我决定报考大学汉语专业，而不是大家期待的法律或者经济学。父母尊重了我的选择。但命运总有自己的安排，几分之差让我再一次面临两难的选择——公费学习其他专业，或者自费学习汉语专业……于是，我们家召开了第一次“中国主题家

庭会议”。最终，父母下定决心，让我作为一个独立的人去尝试着追求属于自己的梦想。我永远爱我的父母，他们是我学习汉语、走向中国的“坚强后盾”。2012 年 9 月，我如愿进入基辅国立语言大学汉语专业学习。

从此，我每天都和“一笔一画”在一起，他们成为连接我和中国的纽带。那时我总是天真地想：多写一笔一画，我就离中国更近一步。一年以后，命运大门第一次正式地为我的梦想打开。2013 年 9 月，中国提出共建“一带一路”的重要倡议，基辅国立语言大学孔子学院就在这一背景下揭牌成立。我有幸成为孔子学院的第一批学员，孔子学院的老师带领、培养、陪伴着我踏上了一个新的学习汉语的征程。

2014 年 9 月至 2015 年 6 月，我获得了孔子学院的奖学金，并且获得了到天津外国语大学留学一年的资格。这是我第一次真正置身汉语母语环境，近距离地体验中国日常生活和习俗文化。一年的留学生活让我大开眼界，收获良多。2016 年 5 月，我登上“汉语桥”世界大学生中文比赛乌克兰赛区的舞台，并且获得第一名，可以代表乌克兰赴华参加全球总决赛。

期间我的中国老师对我开始了新一轮的“全天候培训”和“全方面指导”。2016 年 8 月，我获得总决赛全球亚军、欧洲冠军，并获得了最佳风采奖。我感谢“汉语桥”，它是我学习汉语、走向中国、与世界各国学子相识交流的“幸运之桥”、“友谊之桥”。

2017 年 7 月，我的生活又发生了几个重要转变。首先，我跟我的女朋友——跟我一样热爱汉语和中国文化的乌克兰美女结婚了。而我们的爱情就是在孔子学院一起学习的时候开始的，可以说，是中国和汉语牵起了我们两个人的缘分。就在婚礼第二天，我们收到中国国家汉办的通知：我们两个人被同济大学国际文化交流学院录取！ 9 月，我们一起到中国深造，继续学习汉语，研究我们喜爱的中国文化。

中国是一个美丽的国家，我的国家乌克兰也是一个美丽的国家。我的祖国位于欧亚大陆腹地，是连接东方和西方的“走廊”，是“一带一路”沿线上的重要国家。学习汉语改变和正在改变着我的人生，而“一带一路”倡议则为中国和乌克兰关系的发展提供了更多的可能。我是汉语、孔子学院、“一带一路”倡议的受益者，所以我也要用我的付出和努力来感恩和回馈。我的理想是要为中乌两国友好合作关系的发展做出自己的贡献。我知道，这不只是一个高尚的梦想，更需要我坚持不懈，一点一滴地做起。就像我在学习汉语、走向中国道路上的每一步。

从开始学习汉语到现在，不知已经写过多少汉字。每写下一笔一画，都让我对中国的感情不断加深。而“一带一路”的伟大倡议，则激励着我在未来发展和追逐梦想的道路上不断前行。“一笔一画”将我与中国紧紧相连，“一带一路”让我与梦想热情相拥。让我们一笔一画地共同描绘“一带一路”的美好前程吧！

My Chinese Dream and the Belt and Road

Zvenyhoro Dskyi Pavlo / Ukraine

The International School of Tongji University, Master

The story between me and China is like Chinese characters, drawn out one by one. On the road of learning Chinese and going to China, I can't forget how I went step by step from the past to today.

On my 7th birthday, my family gave me a children's atlas as a gift. That was the first time I found this mysterious country — China on the map. From then on, a little heart gave birth to a big dream — I want to learn her language, understand her history and culture, and continue to explore her mystery. I do not know how many times I have turned the map book. It is old and broken, but I still treasure it until today, because it is my "leader" for learning Chinese and going to China.

Time flies so fast, and soon I graduated from high school, and I faced the first important choice in my life. Yes, I did not give up the dream of ten years buried in my heart. I decided to apply for the university Chinese major, not the law or economics that everyone expected. My parents respected my choice. But destiny always has its own arrangements. Again I had to had face with a dilemma—to study other majors at public expense, or to study Chinese at my own expense...So our family held the first "Chinese-themed family conference". In the end, my parents made up their minds to let me try to pursue my own dream as an independent person. I love my parents forever, they are my "strong supporters" for learning Chinese and moving towards China. In September 2012, I entered the Chinese language major of the Kyiv National Linguistic University as I wish.

Since then, I have been with one drawing every day, and they have become the link between me and China. At that time, I always thought naively: I will be one step closer to China if I write one more stroke. A year later, the lucky gate opened for my dream for the first time. In September 2013, China put forward an important initiative to jointly build the "Belt and Road". The Confucius Institute at Kyiv National Linguistic University was inaugurated in this context. I was fortunate to be the first batch of students of the Confucius Institute. The Confucius Institute has led, cultivated and accompanied me on a new journey of learning Chinese.

From September 2014 to June 2015, I received a scholarship from the Confucius Institute and obtained the qualification to study in Tianjin Foreign Studies University for one year. This is the first time that I am truly exposed to the environment of Chinese as my mother tongue and have a close experience of Chinese daily life and customs. One year's studying abroad has opened my eyes and made me gain a lot. In May 2016, I stepped onto the stage of the Ukraine Division of the "Chinese Bridge" Chinese Proficiency Competition for Foreign College Students and won the first place. I can represent Ukraine in the global finals in China. During this period, my Chinese teacher started a new round of "all-weather training" and "all-round guidance" for me. In August 2016, I won the global runner-up in the finals, the European champion, and won the best style award. I am grateful to the "Chinese Bridge". It is a "lucky bridge" and a "bridge of friendship" for me to learn Chinese, go to China, and communicate with students from all over the world.

In July 2017, there were several important changes in my life. First of all, I got married with my girlfriend, a Ukrainian beauty who also loves Chinese and Chinese culture. And our love started when we were studying together in the Confucius Institute. It can be said that China and Chinese brought us together. On the second day of the wedding, we received a notice from Hanban: We both were admitted to the School of International Cultural Exchange of Tongji

University! In September, we went to China for further studies, continued to learn Chinese together in the same boat, and explored our favorite Chinese culture.

China is a beautiful country, and my homeland, Ukraine, is also a beautiful country. My motherland is located in the hinterland of Eurasia. It is a "corridor" connecting the East and the West. It is an important country along the "Belt and Road". Learning Chinese has changed and is changing my life, and the "Belt and Road" initiative has provided more possibilities for the development of relations between China and Ukraine. I am a beneficiary of Chinese language, Confucius Institutes, and the "Belt and Road" initiative, and a beneficiary of China, so I also want to use my dedication and hard work to thank and give back. My ideal is to make my own contribution to the development of friendly cooperative relations between China and Uzbekistan. I know that this is not just a noble dream, but also requires me to persevere and start bit by bit. It's like every step I take in learning Chinese and walking towards China.

I can hardly count how many Chinese characters have been written since I started learning Chinese. Every time I write a stroke, my feelings for China deepened. The great plan of "Belt and Road" has inspired me to move forward on the road of future development and pursuit of dreams. One stroke and the other closely connects me to China, and the "Belt and Road" initiative allows me to embrace my dreams. Let us make the bright future of the "Belt and Road" together!

汉学家的“中国结”｜我愿变成中约文化使者

［约旦哈希姆王国］茉莉
中国人民大学博士研究生

我是茉莉，来自约旦哈希姆王国，今年 26 岁。2014 年 6 月毕业于约旦大学中文系；2016 年 6 月，硕士毕业于复旦大学汉语国际教育专业；现为中国人民大学国际关系学院外交学系博士生。

在华 4 年中，我深刻感受到自己和中国的缘分。2011 年，我获得了孔子学院奖学金，在湖南大学学习了一年汉语；又于 2014 年、2016 年两度来华学习深造。可以说中国塑造了我，中国培养了我。不仅是在中国，在我的祖国约旦，我也时时刻刻被中国的情谊感染着。2016 年 9 月，我参加了第四届中阿大学校长论坛，在这个会议上，我担任同声传译；同时，我也开始在约旦大学当汉语老师。2017 年春节期间，中国婺剧团来约旦演出，我应中国驻约旦大使馆的邀请担任节目主持人，后来留在大使馆政治部门工作。

在中国的这些年，我不仅收获了知识，还收获了感动。中国不仅给我提供了知识和机遇，更重要的是给了我很多人生的感悟，在此，我和大家分享一个我的留华故事。在来北京读博的第一年，我遇到了很大的麻烦——我长了智齿，非常疼。当时我真的是举目无亲，从约旦带来的药也无济于事。来华之前，BUDDY 项目给我介绍了一个中国语伴，他真的帮了我很多忙。他带我去北大口腔医院，可是我的护照还在中国出入境管理局，不能挂号。我的朋友就带我去约旦大使馆开证明，然后再去医院。要知道，在北大口腔医院要是想挂到专家号就要凌晨一点去排队。他陪我起个大早去排队，最后终于见到了医生，医生说我的牙周情况比较复杂，手术有风险，牙神经有可能被破坏而导致嘴唇失去知觉。当时背井离乡的我一听见这个消息马上就害怕了，也不敢做手术，只想回国。我的中国朋友对我说“姐！虽然我们来自不同的国家，信仰不同的宗教，也说不同的语言，但是我们都是人。我作为你现在唯一认识的中国朋友，我必须好好代表中国人、好好代表我的国家帮助你。姐！我可以让我妈妈来北京陪你做手术！有家人的话也不会那么疼。”当时我真的感谢真主使我选择在北京学习，他把我感动哭了。但是那个时候我还是决定回国做手术。回国之前，他还送我中秋节的礼物，说“这些都是清真的月饼，是我妈妈送给你的，希望你快点恢复。”又说“姐！别忘记和家人一起吃，给他们介绍我们中国的文化。”那时，我心里在想“来了北京留学，我一点都不后悔！感觉北京是我第二个故乡、中国

人民是我的家人！”

来人民大学读博已经一年了，我觉得自己获得了很丰富的知识。我经常参加国际关系学院举办的各类讲座，与导师聊国际问题和中东问题。简而言之，国际关系是指人们超越国家界限建立起来的一种特殊社会关系，包括政治、经济、军事、社会、文化等关系。在人民大学学习过程当中，我阅读了与国际关系专业相关的书籍，掌握了国际关系专业理论和研究方法。同时，我也加强了关于中国政治与中国历史知识的学习和研究，但是中国有五千年的历史，中国政治社会源远流长，在这方面我要继续加强学习。此外，我还了解了国际社会之间的关系，如国家、政府国际组织、非政府国际组织、跨国公司等。除了学术研究以外，我还打算从读博士的第二年起在约旦驻中国大使馆工作。

在中国的时候，有很多人问我关于约旦和其他阿拉伯国家、中国与约旦的关系，中国与约旦在哪些方面有合作等问题。当我向他们解释的时候，他们非常感兴趣。中国和约旦属于不同的文化圈，虽然它们之间有很多不同之处，但是也有很多相同之处。我想通过两个国家的一些方面比较，可以找出两个国家的异同，从而从文化层面上加深中约两国人民的理解和沟通。而我作为一名汉语学习者，无论将来是在中国还是在约旦，我都会从事增进中约两国关系方面的工作，努力成为中约两国的使者，促进两个国家、两个民族的沟通和交流，为了两国人民的未来和福祉而努力。

To be a Cultural Messenger between China and Jordan

Yasmeen Salah / Jordan

Renmin University of China, Ph.D

I am Yasmeen Salah, from the Hashemite Kingdom of Jordan, 26 years old. Graduated from the Chinese Department of Jordan University in June 2014; in June 2016, graduated from Fudan University with a master's degree in Chinese International Education; now I'm a doctoral student in the Department of Diplomacy of the School of International Relations, Renmin University of China.

During the four years of studying in China, I deeply felt that I was really connected with China. In 2011, I won a Confucius Institute scholarship and studied Chinese for a year at Hunan University in Changsha. I came to China for further studies twice in 2014 and 2016. It can be said that China has shaped and cultivated me. Not only in China, but also in my home country, Jordan, I am also constantly infected by China. In September 2016, I participated in the 4th China-Arab University Presidents Forum. At this meeting, I acted as interpreter. At the same time, I also started to be a Chinese teacher at Jordan University. During the 2017 Spring Festival, the Chinese Wu Opera Troupe came to Jordan to perform. At the invitation of the Chinese Embassy in Jordan, I served as the host of the show and then worked in the political department of the embassy.

During these years in China, I have not only gained knowledge, but also gained inspiration. China not only provided me with knowledge and opportunities; more importantly, it gave me a lot of insights in life. Here, I will share with you a story of my staying in China. In the first year of my Ph.D. study in Beijing, I ran into a lot of trouble — I had "toothache" and it hurt very much. I was really unaccompanied at the time, and the medicine brought from Jordan was of no use. Before coming to China, the BUDDY project introduced me to a Chinese language partner who really helped me a lot. He took me to the hospital of Stomatology at Peking University, but my passport was still in the China Exit-Entry Administration, so I could not register. My friend took me to the Jordanian Embassy to issue a certificate, and then I went to the hospital. You know, if you want to get the hospital registration number there, you have to line up at one o'clock in the morning. He woke up early with me to line up, and finally saw the doctor. The doctor said that my periodontal condition was complicated, the operation was risky, and the nerves of the teeth might be damaged and cause loss of consciousness on the lips. When I was leaving my hometown, I became scared as soon as I heard the news. I didn't dare to undergo surgery, I just wanted to go back home. For comforting me, my Chinese partner said, "Sister! I can ask my mother to come to Beijing to accompany you for surgery! It won't hurt so much if you have family members." At that time, I really thanked Allah for making me choose to study in Beijing. He made me deeply moved and cried. But at that time I still decided to return to Jordan for surgery. Before returning to Jordan, he gave me gifts for the Mid-Autumn Festival, said, "These are all halal. My mother gave you moon cakes, I hope you will recover soon." Said again, "Sister! Don't forget to eat with your family and introduce them to our Chinese culture." At that time, I was thinking, I have no regrets when I came to Beijing to study! I feel that Beijing is my second hometown and the Chinese people are my family!

It has been a year since I came to Renmin University to study for a Ph.D. I think I have gained a lot of knowledge. I often participate in various lectures organized by the School of International Relations and chat with my tutors about international issues and Middle East issues. In short, international relations refer to a special social relationship established by people beyond national boundaries, including political, economic, military, social, and cultural relations. In the process of studying at Renmin University, I read books related to international relations and mastered the theory and research methods of international relations. At the same time, I have also strengthened the study and research on Chinese politics and Chinese history. However, China has a history of over 5,000 years and Chinese culture also has a long history. In this regard, I will continue to strengthen my study. In addition, I also learned about the relationship between the international community, such as countries, government international organizations, non-governmental international organizations, multinational companies, etc. In addition to academic research, I also plan to work in the Jordanian Embassy in China from my second year of Ph.D.

When I was in China, many people asked me about the relationship between Jordan and other Arab countries, China and Jordan, and in what ways China and Jordan have cooperation. When I explained to them, they were very interested. China and Jordan belong to different cultural circles. Although there are many differences between them, they also have many similarities. I want to compare some aspects of the two countries to find out the similarities and differences between the two countries, so as to deepen the understanding and communication between the people of China and Jordan from the cultural level. As a Chinese learner, whether I will be in China or Jordan in the future, I will be engaged in the work of enhancing the relations between China and Jordan, and strive to become the messenger of China and Jordan, and promote the communication between the two countries and the two nations. And exchanges, working hard for the future and well-being of the two peoples.

汉学家的“中国结”| 推动中—欧、中—拉加深了解

［德国］安琳娜
巴西利亚大学研究员

我来自德国北部地区，很早就对不同的语言和文化感兴趣。第一次接触关于中国的内容时，我刚从一所地方大学毕业回到家乡，去听了一次报告，主要内容是关于中国技术升级及其与该国高速发展的经济的关联性。从那一刻起，我就决定要去中国看看，要去了解这个国家的文化和社会。

几年后，我在柏林一家专注于亚洲和拉丁美洲市场的咨询公司工作。我的工作涉及投资，合作伙伴包括巴西和中国公司。中国公司可为南半球国家提供的投资范围甚广，包括基础设施，创新和可再生能源等，这些机遇迅速凸显。

我与中国合作伙伴密切合作，决定研究中国这一快速发展的经济体的巨大潜力及其与全球他国关系中扮演的重要角色。自此，我的中国故事拉开序幕。在学术和发展结合的基础上，我于 2015 年在达姆施塔特技术大学和巴西利亚大学获得双博士学位，专注研究中国与德国和巴西的关系。如今，中国是巴西最大的经济伙伴，开展两国关系的比较研究将有助于进

一步加强双方的了解与合作。第二年，我来到北京进行学术研究，被这里的氛围深深地吸引。这里既有深厚历史积淀的过去，也有潜力无限的将来，更有经济发展和技术创新为内核。

中国努力加快社会经济发展以及加强与国际社会的联系让人印象深刻。一到北京，我开始为联合国开发计划署工作，在那里我致力于推行一些可持续发展的方法，依托于“一带一路”倡议和中国提出的其他参与全球治理的相关举措。在联合国的工作使我更加了解，中国是一个重要的国际参与者，同时坚持贸易开放和多边主义原则。

在北京我边工作边攻读博士学位，中国文化和语言丰富了我在北京的时光。我感到很充实，也收获了经验、结交了朋友。离开中国时，我意识到：我的中国故事已经发展成为一种鼓舞人心的体验，涉及个人，专业和学术等多方面。今后，我希望在更广泛的国际关系领域开展工作，推动中—欧与中—拉之间加深了解。最终，如果我们能够相互学习并优势互补，全球化的未来将使我们大家受益。

To Enhance the Relationship between China-Europe and China-Latin America

Alena Profit Pachioni / Germany

University of brasilia, Researcher

Coming from the north of Germany, I early became interested in different languages and cultures. My first encounter with China was as a teenager back home at a local university, when I listened to a lecture on technological upgrading in China and how it related to the rapid growth of the country's economy. At that point I decided I would visit China in the future to learn and about its culture and society.

Years later, I was working for a consulting company with a focus on Asian and Latin American markets in Berlin. My job specifically involved investment promotion and I worked with Brazilian and Chinese companies. The opportunities of Chinese companies' investment could offer to the Southern countries diversely, including infrastructure, innovation and renewable energy, became quickly evident. Working closely with Chinese partners, I decided to focus on the potential of China's unique position as a rapidly developing economy and its relations to other countries. This is where my China story began.

After having worked in academia and development cooperation, I started a double Ph.D. degree at the Technical University of Darmstadt (Germany) and the University of Brasilia (Brazil) in 2015 with a focus on China's relations with Germany and Brazil. Nowadays, China is Brazil's biggest economic partner and to comparatively study the relations between the countries will contribute in further understanding and enhancing their cooperation. The following year, I arrived in Beijing for academic studies and was immediately captivated by this inspiring mixture of a glimpse into yesterday's traditional world and future in progress with economic growth and technological innovation at its core.

It is easy to become impressed by China's efforts to speed up socioeconomic development and with its increased engagement with the international community. Soon after my arrival, I started a job at the United Nations Development Programme, where I contributed to the promotion of sustainable development approaches along the Belt and Road Initiative and other initiatives related to China's engagement in global governance, including the BRICs. Working at the UN increased my understanding of China as a key international player, embracing open trade and multilateralism.

While working and studying for my Ph D., Chinese culture and language filled my days in Beijing. I felt enriched by experiences and friendships I could make. When I left China, I realized that My China Story had developed into an inspirational, personal, professional and academic experience. In the future, I hope to work in the broader field of international relations and contribute to a greater sense of understanding between China-Europe and China-Latin America relations. In the end, a globalized future benefits us all if we are able to learn from each other and understand our complementary benefits.

我人生中重要的部分

[澳大利亚] 范宝文
澳大利亚国立大学，中华全球研究中心

我第一次来中国是在 2005 年，大部分时间都在四川、西藏和云南旅行。尽管那三个月大多在农村和山区，但仍令我大开眼界。此行前，我对中国的宗教和武术感兴趣，并在澳大利亚学习了几年。除了满足我的好奇

心，首次访问中国还为我的生活开辟了新路。

在来中国之前，我只知道怎么说“你好”，所以我来中国的目标之一就是练习普通话。依靠一本短语书，我记住了几个重要的短语，包括学习如何计数，并在生活中加以运用。我的中文很糟糕，但当地人都热情帮助我，于是我发现学习新语言虽然是一种挑战，实际上也非常有趣。

回到澳大利亚后，我立即开始在社区大学学习普通话。我花了 18 个月，初见成效。班上的进度相当缓慢，但我把熟悉中文并记忆音调当作是挑战，这也令我心情愉悦。我对自己充满信心，并热衷于学习更多知识并在澳大利亚国立大学（ANU）攻读了硕士学位。

澳大利亚国立大学历史悠久，是研究中国的好地方。来自世界各地的许多专家在那里学习和交流，图书馆也收藏了大量中英文资源。在两年的学习计划中，我加深了对中国历史和当代社会的理解，尤其是宗教的重要性这方面。我还在台湾继续学了一个学期的普通话，毕业后又继续回那里进一步学习语言。虽然我已花了四年的时间完全沉浸在汉学中，但是我学习得越多，我越渴望学习。中国文化博大精深逐渐展现，我对学习的渴望也与日俱增。

2011 年初，我开始在澳大利亚国立大学新开设的澳大利亚中华全球研究中心（CIW）担任博士研究生，于 2017 年 12 月毕业。我在澳大利亚中华全球研究中心（CIW）的六年时间充满刺激和挑战。除了完成自己对台湾宗教文化史的博士研究之外，我还对电影和中国古代历史也产生了新兴趣。这些年里，我遇到了许多来自世界各地的专家，他们与我分享了知识，让我对中国复杂的历史和迷人的现状有了细致的了解。

2017 年中，我成立了首都学术咨询顾问公司。我现在提供研究和编辑服务，目前与外交部和商务部签约。我撰写了澳中理事会的历史（1978—2018），并帮助一些中国学者规划他们的研究，协助他们把研究成果发表到英文期刊。2017 年，我先后三次回到中国，为未来的合作开展新的研究。我很高兴有机会访问重庆，希望能与当地的专家会面并结交新朋友。过去二十年来，中国一直是我人生中很重要的一部分，我相信它将越来越好。

The Important Part in My Life

Paul James Farrelly / Australia

Australian Centre on China in the World, the Australian National University

I first went to China in 2005 and spent most of that time travelling around Sichuan, Tibet and Yunnan. It was an eye opening three months for me, with a great deal of it spent in rural and mountainous areas. Prior to this trip I was interested in Chinese religions and martial arts, and had studied these for several years in Australia. Beyond being the culmination of years of curiosity, this first visit to China put my life on a new path.

Prior to arriving in China I only knew how to say ' 你好 ' so one of my goals was to practice Mandarin. Equipped with a small phrase book, I memorized several important phrases, including learning how to count, and threw myself into everyday life. My Chinese was terrible, but locals were generally supportive and I found the challenges of this new language to actually be great fun.

Upon returning to Australia, I immediately started studying Mandarin at a community college. I did this for 18 rewarding months. Admittedly, the pace of the class was quite slow but I enjoyed the challenge of becoming familiar with the Chinese script and trying to memorize tones. Feeling confident in my abilities and enthusiastic to learn more, I enrolled in a master's degree at the Australian National University (ANU).

Australian National University (ANU) has a long history as an excellent place to study China. Many experts from all over the world have studied and taught there and the library houses a superb collection of resources in English and Chinese. During the two years of my program I deepened my understanding of Chinese history and contemporary society, especially the importance of religion. I also studied Mandarin in Taiwan for a term and after graduation returned there for 18 months to undertake further language study. By this stage I had spent four years fully immersed in Sinology, yet it seemed the more I studied, the more I realized I had to learn. The layers and complexities of Chinese culture kept revealing themselves to me and my urge to continue learning had not yet faded.

In early 2011 I commenced as a PhD candidate at ANU's newly opened Australian Centre on China in the World (CIW, 中华全球研究中心). Graduating in December 2017, my six years at CIW were stimulating and challenging. In addition to completing my own doctoral research on the cultural history of religion in Taiwan, I fostered new interests in cinema and ancient Chinese history. During these years I met many experts from around the world who have shared their knowledge with me, allowing me to develop a nuanced understanding of China's complex history and fascinating present.

In mid-2017 I established a consultancy called Capital Academic Advisory (首都学术咨询). Offering research and editing services, I am currently contracted to the Department of Foreign Affairs and trade to write the history of the Australia China Council (澳中理事会) (1978-2018) and have helped a number of Chinese academics prepare their research for publication in English language journals. In 2017 I returned to China on three separate occasions, conducting new research and developing networks for future collaboration. I am excited about the opportunity to visit Chongqing where I hope to meet local experts and make new friends. China has been a massive part of my life for the last twenty years and I am sure it will continue to be well into the future.

我的求学经历

［布隆迪］龚泽马

贝宁阿波美卡拉维大学兼职教师

我是龚泽马，来自布隆迪共和国，我的家乡在布隆迪中南部瑞安索罗区。1975 年 9 月 20 日，我出生在一个由 9 个孩子组成的家庭。我有一个温暖而快乐的童年，我的母亲非常和善慈爱，而我的父亲为了维持生计在

首都布琼布拉工作。

1981 年 9 月，我六岁时在瑞安索罗小学开始接受小学教育。记得当时，是我主动提出，才开始上小学，那时父母认为上学还为时过早，但我成功地说服了瑞安索罗小学校长，也是我的叔叔利布瓦尔老师。因为那时我们村庄没有托儿所，感觉很无聊，所以我每天都很高兴去学校学习和社交。

上小学之后，我给老师和同学们留下了深刻的印象。因为一直到小学毕业，我都是班里的第一名。小学期间，有一个非常严峻的考验，就是只有小部分成绩比较优异的孩子才能上初、高中一体的学校。大家都必须参加全国性的统考，只有 10% 的幸运小学生通过考试后去州立寄宿学校。

我是幸运的，十二岁的我，进入了马塔纳区的鲁班加初中，它是一所寄宿学校，除了在休假期间，我必须留在学校。在鲁班加初中，我依旧保持了良好成绩，直到初中毕业，我始终是班上的第一名。初中学习期间，我是青春期的少年，虽然我学习非常好，但因为有时会挑战老师的权威，他们对我不是很满意。我受到了很多警告，如果不是我的数学老师去帮我说情，我还差点被学校开除了。他们决定不开除我，但要求我在初中毕业后转入另一所学校。

1991 年 9 月，我进入离家乡不远的基特加省的吉舒比高中读书，我的表现依旧出色，并被安排到了学校的科学部门。然而，1993 年 10 月，在我高中的最后一年时，我国的第一位民主派候选人被暗杀，导致政治动乱和内战，这影响了我们的生活和学习。

吉舒比高中被激进分子包围，他们想替被害者报复现任总统，但他们的攻击目标却是无辜的百姓，尽管当时我们并不真正了解我们国家政治的根本和隐藏的面貌。当受到威胁我打电话给学术总监时，对方建议我们退出吉舒比地区，前往和平的马塔纳区。我对这个地区非常了解，于是我带领我的 400 名同学，安全抵达了马塔纳区寻求庇护。教育部决定把我送回我以前的鲁班加高中，在那里我再次见到了我以前的同学，一起学习，并保持班级第一名的成绩，直到 1994 年毕业。

毕业几个月后，我去了布琼布拉，并在布隆迪大学医学院就读。我喜欢布琼布拉的学习环境，我的许多亲戚在业余时间经常来看我并为我提供一些零食。但是这个国家处于战争状态，反叛分子正在挑战当时的军队，有时当我们从学校出来时，他们正在交火。

就像命中注定，我躺在布隆迪大学穆坦加校园的床上，听到布隆迪电台的通知：那些有意愿获得中国奖学金的学生可以去教育部注册并于 1995 年 2 月 28 日参加考试。听到通知的第二天，我去了教育部总部，提交了所需的文件并准备考试，其中包括数学、物理和化学。

这是很多人梦寐以求的机会，大使馆只需要六名学生，但报名考试的有三百多人。我满怀信心地参加考试，并继续进行医学学习，对此前的考试并未过多在意。1995 年 6 月，我被邀请到中国驻布隆迪大使馆领取我的签证申请表和录取通知书。这一刻我相信，这次的旅程正在变得真实，并告知我的近亲，我即将离开家乡去中国留学。

然而那时候，受西方宣传的影响，许多布隆迪人认为成功的唯一途径是在比利时、法国或美国，他们对中国了解不多，因此不鼓励我去那里。可我意识到当时布隆迪的局势并不稳定，我不想放弃这次机会，我对自己说，试试看。

1995 年 9 月 3 日，我们途径布鲁塞尔、巴黎来到北京。尽管我只是一个来自布隆迪贫穷国家的乡村男孩，但巴黎和布鲁塞尔的城市建筑并没有让我印象深刻，我只记住了北京首都的辉煌灿烂。在北京的两天，我感受到了北京人的谦虚和睿智。之后我来到了南京师范大学，接受了一年的汉语训练。

中国是一个多元文化和多民族的国家，南京亦是一座非常美丽的城市，有着友善的人民，在那个特别的城市里，我遇到了我的中国朋友潘。她是我见过最美丽和有爱心的人，她向我学习法语，并教我学习中国语言。

1996 年，我不得不离开南京，前往无锡江南大学，开始我的专业学习。最开始我学习的专业是食品工程。但是，我不太喜欢这个专业。这时我遇到了顾老师，他曾经在贝宁担任外交官，他对非洲人非常友好并且尊重，在他的帮助下，我被录取并进入信息与控制工程学院的计算机科学系。

坦率地说，在中国学习非常不容易；中国学生的基础教育比我们更扎实。尽管我认为自己有较强的学术能力，但这时我开始怀疑自己，因为一切都显得太困难，尤其在数学学习上。我挣扎着、努力着，我知道，在没有取得学位的情况下回到布隆迪会让父母非常失望，因为他们总是对我有很大的期望。

因为语言障碍，我每天都要去中国朋友宿舍寻求帮助。在我的生命中，寻求同学对我进行学术帮助的情况是非常罕见的，因为当我在布隆迪时，大部分同学都崇拜并且尊敬我，因为我能够给他们一些学习帮助。这种情况让我感觉非常沮丧。

但是，我慢慢地成长起来，我的努力甚至得到了老师的肯定。几乎每年的 10 月 1 日（中国国庆节），我都被外国学生办公室授予奖励，以表彰我在大学期间的学习成绩和行为。经过我的不懈努力，我在 2000 年获得了外国留学生奖学金，这使我能够继续攻读计算机科学硕士学位，而不必返回布隆迪。

除了语言障碍，另一个障碍是资金的短缺。那时候我们的奖学金是不够买飞机票回国探亲的。因此我会在周末参加音乐会，挣得零用钱，也可以算是丰富生活体验。我还为我的大学开发了网站，虽然它不是一个很完善的设计，但是学校依然将它采纳为支持项目，并给予奖励。

为了能够有足够的资金回到布隆迪，我决定在光华私立学校当高中老师，每月能获得 800 美元左右的收入，我在两年的时间内攒了 12000 美元。

2005 年我回到了家乡，成为计算机科学课程大学讲师。当我进入布隆迪大学时，学校要求拥有博士学位，所以我在中国驻布隆迪大使馆的帮助下，成功申请了奖学金，并于 2014 年被湖南大学录取。而现在，我刚刚提交了我的论文，还在等待博士毕业。

在中国，我有机会参观这个美丽的国家的许多地方，主要在东部和南部。我不得不承认，中国是世界上最幸运的国家之一，在国家领导人的正确领导及其远见下，中国人民团结起一切可以团结的力量并利用一切可利用的资源。

从东到西，从南到北，我经历了几乎相同的城市建筑，只有微小的差异。可是美丽的风景，平原和山脉、绿地、湖泊等旅游景点还是值得一游的。

中国人，不论是政治家还是普通人，都非常信守承诺，这是如今罕见的品质。我想这是他们能够取得成功的主要原因。他们提倡维护世界和平与全球稳定，虽然他们有许多道德标准不属于任何宗教，但仍然值得学习和借鉴。

我对中国有很多好的回忆。在这里，我学到了很多东西，不仅是中国语言与文化，还有计算机科学与技能，大大地提高了我的生活技能和社会地位。

虽然我从没有用物质礼物赠予我的大学老师和中国政府，但我真诚感激他们的努力，他们帮助我们这样的发展中国家，相信我们、尊重我们，给我们学习和与他们一起成长的机会。当我们在中国学习时，为我们提供保护。他们没有义务帮助我们，但他们作为有强烈责任心的政府，一直在为人类的团结而努力。

现在，我们国家也有同样的信念，在积极开展国际合作，为实现世界和平，人类稳定和可持续发展，让这个世界变得更加美好而努力。

My Study Experience

Hilaire Nkunzimana / Burundi
University of Abomey-Calavi, Part-time Teacher

My name is Hilaire Nkunzimana and my Chinese name is "龚泽马". Native of Burundi Republic, in the Central south part of my country, precisely in the Ryansoro District, I was born on 20th, September, 1975 in a family of nine children.I had a modest but happy childhood with a very caring and loving mother on my side while my father was busy working in the capital city Bujumbura, looking for financial means to ensure our Education and our well-being.

I started my primary school in September 1981, at Ryansoro Primary School at the age of six like other children of my county. I started my primary school as a result of my own initiative because my parents thought it was too early to go to school but I successfully convinced my uncle Liboire who was Ryansoro Primary School principal and teacher at that time.

I was very happy to go to school and socialize because I was very bored and during that time there was no nursery school in my village. After I began my primary school, I impressed my teachers and my classmates as I succeeded to be always the first of my class since my first year until my completion of my primary school.During my time, there was a very difficult test giving access to secondary education within my own country. It was a national exam; state-organized and only 10% of lucky primary pupils could go to state boarding schools after passing that exam.

It was rare for pupils to pass that national exam without having to repeat once or multiple times.I was among the rare ones and I was oriented to Rubanga High school, in Matana District, not far from my home district.

At the age of twelve, I left my village, and entered a boarding school where I have to stay at school except during vacations. At Rubanga High School, I also performed very well keeping my record of being always the first of my class until I completed my Junior High School. But when I was in 9th form of my Junior high school, I was a teenager, although I was performing very well in my class, my teachers were not always satisfied with me because I wanted sometimes to challenge them.So I received many warnings until I was almost dismissed from my school if it was not the implication of my former math teacher who convinced the rest of his colleagues to back their decision.They accepted not to expel me but suggested to redirect me to another school after Junior high school.

After the 10th of my junior high school, it was in September 1991, I integrated Gishubi High school, in Gitega Province, which is also located not far from my home town.Arrived in Gishubi High school, my performance was also very good and kept my top rank of my entire class and was directed in Scientific Section of my High school.

In October 1993, which is the final year of high school, the first democratic candidate of my country was assassinated resulting in political unrest and civil war which did not spare our boarding schools.

Our Gishubi High school were surrounded by militants who wanted to revenge the killed president and we were targeted innocent although at that time we didn’t really understand the underlying and hidden face of our country politics. Threatened, I called the academic director and suggested that we quit the Gishubi Place and walk towards Matana District which was more peaceful. As a person who knew very well the region, I guided all 400 students of my institution and all arrived in Matana District safe and sought for refuge. We left behind all our belongings and the ministry of Education decided to send me to my former school of Rubanga High school where I met again my former classmates, studied together and kept my first rank of my class until I graduated from Rubanga high school on November first, 1994.

Few months after my graduation, I went to Bujumbura and was admitted in Burundi University in Medical school. I liked my new study environment as in Bujumbura, there were many of my relatives who often came to see me and offer some drinks during my spare time.

But the country was at war, the rebels were challenging the then Army and sometimes we were at cross-fire of the belligerents when we were coming off from our lessons.

Just like a God's Plan, I was lying on my bed at Mutanga Campus of Burundi University, after a tiring review of my lessons when I heard a notice from Burundi Radio that Students who are willing to get Chinese Scholarship can go to the Ministry of Education to register and that the selection test is due on February 28th, 1995.

After hearing that notice, I went the next day to the ministry of Education headquarters, submitted the required documents, and went on preparing my test which covered mathematics, physics and chemistry. When the day arrived, I went to sit for the exam, confident of course, although we were many seeking for that opportunity.

Let's mention that we were over three hundred appliants when the Embassy only wanted six.

After the test, we were not informed about the results until May, 1995 and I continued with my medical studies as nothing had happened.

In June, 1995, I was invited to the Chinese Embassy in Burundi to receive my visa application form and my admission notice. Then I began to believe that this journey to China is coming true and informed my close relatives about my imminent departure to study in China.I have to admit that at that time many Burundians didn't know much about China and some were discouraging me to go there. Western propaganda has corrupted their mind and thought that the only way to success in life is to study in Belgium, France or America. But after a personal analysis, I came to realize that Burundi situation at that time was not ideal, and some information from Chinese Embassy gave me some insight and I said to myself, let me try and see.

On September 3rd, 1995, we took SABENA airlines going first to Belgium, where I stayed in Sodehotel, in Woluwe District at the cost of airlines. We stayed there for two days before embarking Air France and went for Paris just for transit waiting for Air China leading us to Beijing. Let me just mention that although I was just a village boy and coming from Burundi poor country, Bruxelles didn't impress me at all with its old city architecture compared to Paris where I witnessed the real modern world.

Arrived in Beijing, although it was in 1995, I was impressed by the greatness of the capital city of the Middle Empire. Humble people but intellectually sound-that was the first impression I got from Beijing institute Managers where we stayed for two days before embarking the train which took me to Nanjing Normal University. I stayed for one year, being trained in Mandarin there. When I arrived in Nanjing, I was accommodated at Nanshan Hotel, a multicultural and multiracial environment. It was not China only, but it was the entire world that I came to meet and experience. Nanjing is a very beautiful city with friendly people, where I first met my Chinese friend, Pan. She made my stay in China more bearable, and I have to admit, I learned from her many things starting from Chinese Language but also some daily life tips. She was modern, beautiful and caring person that I have ever met. She also learned French from me, and this shaped her destiny as now she is married to a French national after impressing him with very fluent French.

In 1996, I had to leave Nanjing and head to Wuxi, now known as Jiangnan University, where I had to begin with my major studies. Before I had to do food engineering, I didn't really like this major, that's why I get the help from late Gu. He used to serve as Diplomat in Benin and was more friendly to Africans. As he knew us more than anyone, he treated me very well with respect, and helped me in many circumstances including in assisting me to change my specialty. I was then admitted into the school of Information and Control engineering, in the department of Computer Science. To be frank, to study in China is not very easy; the Chinese students are better prepared to embrace their university studies than us. With different backgrounds, although I had a very high esteem regarding my academic abilities, sometimes I started to doubt about myself, because everything appeared too difficult, even mathematics which was the best when I was in Burundi. But I struggled; I knew that returning to Burundi without a degree will sound like a shame and betrayal to my parents who always counted on me.

With the language barrier, one year of Chinese Language training, was not enough to be put at the same level and compete with my Chinese classmates. That's why I had to go almost on daily basis to go to Chinese friends dormitory to seek for their help. It was something rare in my life to go to seek for my classmates help regarding the academic affairs because when I was in Burundi, the situation was reverse since most of my Burundi classmates admired me and respected me due to the academic help and assistance I was giving them when I was in Burundi. I knew that when I was in Burundi, many girls wanted to make friends with me to secure their class advancement but it was not the case when I was in China anymore. This situation frustrated me so much that I developed a dependence on others in order to study.

But gradually, I managed to achieve, and even my educators recognized my efforts so much that almost every October 1st, Chinese National Holiday, I was granted an award by the foreign student's office in recognition of my academic performance and behavior at our University. It is thanks to my performance and good conduct that I got the excellent foreign student's Scholarship in 2000 which allowed me to continue with my master degree in computer science without having to return to Burundi. Another hindrance to my happiness while in China, worth to mention, that time was insufficient funds which deprived me the right to visit my family for five continuous years of my studies. As a matter of fact, I could not afford the plane ticket, and I missed too much my family that I nearly got depressed. The scholarship during my time was 550 yuan, which could only cover food and garments. Other students from other countries were having supplementary scholarship from their respective countries, which was not the case for me due to economic capacity of my government.

Despite that financial constraint, I managed to overcome it as I was attending some musical concerts, sometimes performing some entertainment dances, to get some pocket money on weekend, which revealed also to be an enriching experience. I developed also the website for my university, although it was not a very good design, it was adopted by the university as a sign of support and they rewarded me with some pocket money and I was grateful for giving me that opportunity.

After my master degree graduation, I knew that going back to Burundi without financial means will turn into a nightmare, so I decided to stay as high school teacher at Guanghua private school where I gained monthly around 800 dollars.It was enough and I managed to save up to 12000 dollars in two years. But I was always not happy with my situation because I knew I am worth more than that.

I returned then back home in 2005 and began my professional journey mainly as university lecturer of computer science courses. When I integrated Burundi University, the requirement was to have a PhD degree, so with the help of Chinese Embassy in Burundi, I successfully applied for a scholarship and was admitted at Hunan University in 2014. I just rounded up my thesis and I am still waiting for my doctoral graduation.

While in China, I have had the opportunity to visit many parts of this beautiful country but mainly the eastern and southern part of China. I have to admit that China is one of the most blessed countries on the earth with many resources and many people, who are united under unique leadership and vision; this is my description I can make about China.

From east to west, north to south, I have experienced almost the same city architecture, with minor differences. Beautiful

landscapes, plain land and mountains, green lands, natural and artificial lakes, many scenic spots are worth to be visited at least once in one's life. Chinese people, being politicians or common people, keep their promise and their word, which is a rare quality that we can still find in today's world folks. That's why I guess their business success mainly stems from those basic principles and character that they still possess. Their moral standards, although, many of which are not affiliated to any creed, are worth being referenced and followed to sustain world peace and global stability.

My stay in china can be portrayed by ups and downs, good experiences and bad ones, but to sum up, I had more good experience than bad ones. I learned a lot, not only Chinese Language and Culture, but also Computer Science and Skills, which helped me to upgrade to another level my living standard. For that reason, although I don't have material gifts to give to my former teachers and Chinese government, I want to formally recognize their efforts to assist less privileged people like us for having given us opportunity to learn from them, to live with them, to trust us and offer us protection during our stay in their home land. They had no obligations to help us but they did it as responsible Government, with the strong belief, I guess that we all share the common humanity, and that we are called to assist each other under the cause of human solidarity.We appeal them to continue, in their scope of their means, until poverty and ignorance are totally banned from our planet.

We share the same belief that it is under active international cooperation, people to people exchange, that the world peace, stability and sustainable development will be achieved and make this world a better place to live.

中国文化改变了我的生活

［意大利］李蕊

卡塔尼亚大学终身教授讲师

要说我与中国的渊源，就要从我的小学说起了。一次偶然的机会，父母带我去附近一家中餐馆吃饭。尽管坐落于佛罗伦萨市中心，但从餐厅的风格、陈设、服务员等方面能明显感受到差别。当然最主要的是菜单上多

了些看不懂的文字：中文。这让我觉得非常的新奇，那天的菜品也给我留下了深刻印象。我还记得那家餐厅的服务员是中国人，他还教了我写餐厅的名字“南京”。自此，我开始对那些当时我认为像画画一样的文字产生了兴趣。于是一有机会我便去中国商店购买那些标有中文的食品，关注那些写有中文的商品。那个年代，少有意大利人去中国商店买东西，因此大多中国商店的服务员都认识我，于是我也和那家中国餐馆的服务员成了朋友，他们对我也非常友好并教我更多的中文，尽管当时我并没能理解得很透彻。提及与中文或者中国人更深一步的接触，就要回顾中学时期。那时，班上来了一个中国女孩，可能因为我会写几个汉字，我们很快便成了很要好的朋友，几乎每天在一起上学，放学。只要是在一起，我就会问她关于中国和中文的事。我还记得她教我算数，教我说“我叫 Lavinia”等简单的中文，也正因为如此，让我对这个国家产生了更浓厚的兴趣，也下定了决心将来一定要进一步接触一下这个国家的人民和文化。

2000 年我高中毕业以后就选择去荷兰学习英语，回国后我对将来的学业有了清楚的规划，因此决定在罗马大学读中文。2003 年因北京外国语大学欢迎罗马大学的学生自费去中国学习，我就去北京学了三个月的汉语。我也如愿以偿地来到了这个让我倍感亲切的中国。回国后，较系统地学习了中文便顺利结业。当时我已经发现已无法自拔地爱上了中国，于是我毅然决然地回到了北京。2006 年，我以优异的成绩获得奖学金，在北京语言大学继续学习中文，也正式开启了我在中国为时 6 年的留学生涯。语言大学的课程还未开始，我在意大利驻华使馆的文化处实习了三个月。意大利驻华使馆坐落在北京的三里屯，这也是外国年轻人聚集的地区。我清楚地记得，为了能够更好地学习中文、了解中国文化，我不住在使馆附近，反而搬到了位于北京市中心的交道口。那里紧邻鼓楼、安定门、地安门、雍和宫以及故宫，既是北京历史最悠久地区，也是文化最发达的地方。我住进了老头老太太都住过的平房、小院儿，每天最开心的就是可以接触到老北京的生活，每天都会看路边的大爷们下棋、打扑克、麻将，和大妈聊天。我很快习惯了北京人的方式，北京人也很快接受了我这个西方人。因此，我的口语水平迅速提高，但仅口语好还不够，我立志要看懂更多的汉字。

说起来，汉字是我爱上中国文化最重要原因之一。我还记得上大学时，我发现了某些西方学者有一种奇怪的观点，认为随着语言文字的发展趋势，汉字也会趋于简单化、拼音化，甚至认为汉字是即将被淘汰的“落后文字”。如今，我们都明白可能因为这些学者对人类语言文字的历史有所误解，还可能因为有些人未能意识到汉字对中国思维和中国文化的重要作用。现在，已为人师的我，经常告诉学生，中国古代文人无一例外，皆用竹制毛笔蘸墨书写，笔走龙蛇。笔、墨、纸、砚堪称中国传统文化最重要的工具。这所谓的“文房四宝”对当时文人而言，必不可少。且文人书法和绘画的魅力不仅在于其技法的独特性，熟读中文经典后甚至可以学而优则仕。于是，我总鼓励学生多练字。

学生时代，我每天在练口语的同时还要拼命地写、记汉字，理解汉字意义。我尽可能多去买东西，和北京人聊天，问他们问题。尽管有时我能看出他们些许不耐烦，但我不在意，因为我的目的就是要学好中文。不仅如此，我知道北京人非常喜欢传统艺术，所以我经常会去茶馆，在那里可以欣赏北京的传统艺术，比如相声、评书、京剧、曲艺等。虽然我当时并不能完全听懂这些，但是那种氛围让我记忆犹新，流连忘返。因为我深深地明白一个道理，那就是想学好一个地方的语言，首先要了解这个地方的历史与文化。就这样，我在中国，按照中国人的方式生活着，而这种方式变成了我日常生活习惯。直到现在，睡觉之前都会听我在手机里下载的郭德纲单口相声和评书。

2007 年我考上了清华大学的博士，梦想终于起航。已积累几年的中国文化和汉语经验对我现在的学业很有帮助。因此，我找到了让自己最感兴趣的课题——《中国古代公案小说》，于是我便开始了相关研究。2011 年在罗钢教授和王宁教授的辅导下，我终于拿到清华的博士学位。

毕业以后，因签证的原因我不得不回国，得知这一消息的时候，我伤心得哭起来，但我并未失去对中国文化的浓厚兴趣。一回国，我就申请就读卡塔尼亚大学并被成功录取。我也成为卡塔尼亚大学外语系中国语言与文化课程的资深讲师。在意大利，资深讲师近似美国的副教授职位，所以我一边继续进行我感兴趣的研究课题，不仅主持中文系、讲授中国语言与文学课程、帮学生选择研究课题，同时也忙于对学生论文结构以及其他方面提供综合指导。我所写的文章大多与中国古代公案文学有关，但我也对其他的主题感兴趣。最近我还出版了一本书，叫《中国古代罪案故事》(http://www.aracneeditrice. it/index.php/pubblicazione.html? item=9788825506877)。我回国近七年，每天都忙于上述事务。尽管有时分身乏术，忙不过来，但也乐于为之奉献。中国文化改变了我的生活，我把这看成像俄罗斯套娃一般，里面套着很多有趣又值得研究的话题，让我不断深受启发。

Chinese Culture Changed My Life

Lavinia Benedetti / Italy

University of Catania, Tenure Track Lecturer

The original relation between China and I can go back to my primary school. My parents took me to a nearby Chinese restaurant for a meal. Though it was located in the center of Florence, it differed obviously in style, decoration and service. Especially there were Chinese characters on its menu that I couldn't understand. These Chinese characters made me amazed about them and the dishes we ordered impressed me a lot. I can remember the waiters in this restaurant were Chinese who taught me how to write the name of the restaurant — "南京". From then on, I became interested in the Chinese characters which were like being drawn. Once I had chance , I would go to purchase and focus on the food and goods which were labeled with Chinese characters. At that time, not many Italians went shopping in Chinese stores, so most of the Chinese waiters knew me. Certainly I made friends with the waiters in that restaurant, who were kind to me and taught me much Chinese although I couldn't understand so thoroughly. As far as further contact with Chinese or Chinese people were concerned, it can go back to my middle school period when a Chinese girl came to our class. Maybe because I could write several Chinese characters, we became good friends quickly. We almost went to school and returned home together. As long as we stayed together, I would ask her about Chinese. I can still remember that she taught me how to calculate and say simple Chinese like "I am Lavinia." For this reason, I became more interested in China, and made a decision that I would have closer contact with Chinese people and Chinese culture in future.

After graduation from high school, I chose to learn English in Netherlands in 2000. I knew clearly that what I would study in the future after coming back. Then I decided to major in Chinese in Rome University. In 2003, Beijing Foreign Studies University welcomed the students from Rome University to study in China, and I studied Chinese in Beijing for three months. I finally came to exciting China which I had earnestly dreamed for a long time. After returning to Italy, I finished completion successfully through a period of systematic studies. I found that I had fallen in love with China irrepressibly so I came back to China resolutely. I got the scholarship with excellent grades and studies Chinese in Beijing Language and Culture University in 2006. Then my 6-year study life in China started. Before the language course, I worked as a three-month intern in the cultural department of the Italian embassy in China. The Italian embassy is located in Sanlitun, Beijing, which is also part of a gathering of foreign youths. I clearly remembered that in order to learn Chinese and understand Chinese culture better , I did not choose to live near the embassy. Instead I moved to Jiao Daokou, which was adjacent to the Drum Tower, AnDingmen, Di Anmeng, the Lama Temple and the Forbidden City. That area is most historic area in Beijing and also the place with the most advanced culture. The place which I lived in was the bungalow, small courtyard which the old man old lady once lived in. The happiest thing in my daily life was to have access to the old Beijing life.I can not only see the grandpas play chess, cards and Mahjong by the roadside,but also chat with the aunts. I soon got used to the Beijingers' way, and the Beijingers quickly accepted me as a westerner. That's why my oral Chinese improved so fast. But I held the view that it was not enough to have the ability to speak English and I must understand more Chinese characters.

When I looked back those days, Chinese characters are one of the main reasons for loving Chinese culture. Some western researchers held a weird idea that Chinese characters would be simplified and alphabetization according to the development tendency of characters. Even some regarded Chinese characters as backward characters which would be eliminated soon. Now we all know that these researchers perhaps misunderstood the history of human language, yet some can not fully understand the importance of Chinese characters for Chinese thinking and Chinese culture. Now, as a teacher, I always tell my students that ancient Chinese literati shared one common point without exception-they all used a set of writing brush and ink, wrote unique brush stroke, licked the ink and presented a full page with black and vivid characters. The most important tools of Chinese traditional culture are writing brush, ink stick, ink slab and paper. The so-called Four Treasures of the Study were the necessity of ancient Chinese literati at that time.Moreover, the special charm of writing and paintings was not only unique, and literati who were acquainted with Chinese ancient classics could be selected as officials.In this way I persuade my students to practice writing.

When I was a student, I practiced oral Chinese and at the same time I also made every effort to write and memorize Chinese characters and understand the meaning of Chinese characters. I seized every chance to practice Chinese like going shopping, talking to Beijing people and asking them questions.What's more, I knew that Beijingers like traditional art very much, so I often went to tea house, where I can see the traditional art forms of Beijing, such as crosstalk, storytelling, Peking Opera, Chinese folk art forms and so on. Though I didn't fully understand it, the atmosphere was fresh and unforgettable. Because I understand that you must learn about the culture and the history of the place if you would like to learn the language of it. I lived here in a Chinese way and this way became my daily habits.Until now, I will listen to Guo Degang's monologue comic talk and storytelling downloaded on my mobile phone before going to bed.

In 2007, my dream started to bloom after I had an opportunity to study for my doctor's degree at Tsinghua University. The experience of Chinese culture and Chinese language that I had learned before is very helpful to my study. In that case, I found the subject that I was most interested in is called Chinese Ancient Crime Novel. Then I started my journey of research.With the help of Professor Luo Gang and Wang Ning, I got the doctor's degree eventually.

After graduation, I had to return to homeland because of visa. At the news I cried sadly, but I did not lose the interest in Chinese culture. As soon as I got back to Italy, I applied for the University of Catania. I was accepted and hired as a senior lecturer of Chinese Language and Culture by the Department of Foreign Languages. In Italy, a senior lecturer is generally equivalent to an associate professor in the United States. At this university, I carried on my research work, was in charge of Chinese Department gave Chinese language and culture classes and helped students to choose programs. Meanwhile I was busy with offering help on their thesis structure and other comprehensive guidance. Although most of the articles I wrote are related to ancient Chinese literature, but I am also interested in other topics. Recently I published a book called Chinese Ancient Crime Stories, (http://www.aracneeditrice. it/index.php/pubblicazione. html?item=9788825506877) I have been busy with these things every day for seven years since I came back to Italy. Even though there are so many things to do. But I can say that this job is really what I want in my lifetime. So, Chinese culture changes my life, and I see it as a Russian doll, with lots of interesting and valuable topics, from which I am constantly inspired.

我的中国研究之路

［印度］李天宇
圣雄甘地大学国际关系与政治关系研究学者

一位来自印度小镇的七岁小男孩与他的叔叔一起观看了一部名为《蛇形刁手》的电影，并回到了家中。在众多他所观看的电影中，仅有这一部电影让他陷入了沉思。即使在一两个星期后，他仍在思考着这部电影所传

递的全新文化。他不仅对功夫印象深刻，而且对那部电影中的人物、语言和文化更加好奇，但他知道这部电影是关于中国文化的。经过漫长的努力，他终于成功地租到了一台黑白电视机和录像机，通过一遍又一遍地观看《蛇形刁手》和其他电影录像带，试图来了解中国。

那个七岁的男孩就是我。之后，我便开始阅读中国故事，并通过了解中国绘画和音乐来理解中国文化。在我有限的资源条件内，我一直热衷于了解中国的文化、语言以及整个民族。从 1990 年开始到现在，电影在我对中国文化的具象化理解中起到了重要的作用，这其中更多的是我自己在脑海中所创造的关于中国的浪漫形象。但是后期的书籍和其他读物让我更加清晰地了解了中国的文化和历史。出于同样的好奇心，我决定开始研究国际关系，以便更多地了解文化和历史，尤其是中国历史。在我的学习过程中，没有其他文化可以像中华文明和文化那样不断地激励着我，激发我对知识的渴求。我以中国的黄河文明和丝绸之路的历史为切入点开始了我对中国的研究。

自从人类开始群居生活，并以生存为目的从一个地方迁移到另一个地方，这就已经产生了文明。并且在这个过程中，每个族群都形成了自己的文化，这其中包括生存、定居、狩猎、艺术、思想和工程等。众所周知，世界各地有不同的文明，例如美索不达米亚文明，埃及文明，黄河文明，希腊文明，印度河流域文明等，但黄河文明引起了我的关注。

《史记》和《竹书纪年》描述了 4000 年前的中华文明，并且记载了夏王朝（公元前 2000 年—公元前 1600 年），商朝（公元前 1600 年—公元前 1550 年）和周王朝（公元前 1050 年—公元前 200 年）三个历史上统治黄河流域的朝代。公元前 221 年秦国巩固了对该地区内其他小国的统治，建立了一个庞大的帝国，秦始皇由此统一了中国并且成为历史上的第一位皇帝。在那个时期，为了扩大贸易和财富，亚历山大帝王的统治范围已经扩大到了印度，但是没有出征中国，因为它独特的文化和神秘的地形。

丝绸之路自公元前 12 世纪就已经被发现，汉代时，西方探险家将中国领土标记为“赛里斯国”。汉代实行跨边境的贸易文化。在此期间，张骞被汉武帝派遣出使西域，后来这条线路向北发展成为欧亚地区的古代丝绸之路。有证据表明，汉代时期丝绸大量生产并且被运送到其他地方进行贸易往来。造纸术的发明彻底改变了古代的边境贸易，丰富了丝绸贸易。马帮和商人利用这条线路进行商品交易，使得彼此间的想法得到了交流。中国的产品，例如丝绸、茶叶、瓷器、纸张、火药和铁器在印度、阿拉伯半岛、中东、非洲和欧洲之间流通。

1937 年中国遭到日本侵略，日本屠杀了 1400 多万中国人。这场侵华战争长达八年，无辜的儿童和男女在大规模的轰炸中失去生命，世界历史上最大的屠杀事件之一就发生在中国南京，当我阅读到日本在南京制造大屠杀的这段历史时，我感到无比的恐惧。但中国浴火重生，在毛主席的领导下，1949 年中华人民共和国成立了。

2013 年 3 月 14 日习近平出任中华人民共和国主席后，中国达到了现代发展的黄金时代。“一带一路”倡议是中国国家主席习近平 2013 年提出的一个创新理念，其重点是国际贸易和文化关系的范式转变。这一理念的独特之处在于将不同的文化和贸易联结在一起，以互相学习和互利的和平世界为中心去创造多元化的世界。除了国际组织和各国之间的多边或三边关系之外，一带一路的倡议是中国未来的全球愿景，也是一个中国为构建全球和平关系的一个重要桥梁，这个倡议将连接这个地区的 60 个国家。

目前的国际体系造成了国与国之间的巨大差距，一些国家在全球贸易和文化领域变得越来越不重要。但是习近平主席的远见为所有国家的发展和繁荣提供了平台。当今，即使是西方超级大国，在经济增长、出口商品、建筑业、就业机会以及繁荣发展和人民生活方面都无法与中国竞争。

我们可以说，一个人如果不使用中国制造的茶品就无法完成他的一天。从小型产品到巨型产品，我们无法想象中国生产的技术及其产品的多样性。从印度的一个街头小贩到美国的大型商业公司，都在中国制造和创意的帮助下开展业务，所以今天的中国在全球发展中扮演着至关重要的角色。

我的中国故事讲述了我对中国的好奇以及我对中国历史、文化和文明的了解旅程。这些总能鼓舞我去挖掘并了解令人着迷的关于中国的一切。几千年的历史文化，令人诧异的艺术作品数量、繁荣的文明，这一切从未衰落和消失。这是一段了解中国的地理、艺术、语言、文化、音乐、绘画、手工艺品、文化的交互影响以及宗教的多样性的旅程。根据多年来我对中国的了解，我认为中国文明和文化是世界上最富有的，当代中国是世界上强大的国家之一。

My Study about China

Muhammed Thalhath M. / India

School of International Relations and Politics, Mahatma Gandhi University, Researcher

A seven year old little boy from a small town in India, who watched a movie called *Snake in the Eagle Shadow* with his uncle and went back to home. But it was not as many movies he watched before or after, he got stuck somewhere. Even after one or two weeks he was thinking about the movie he watched about a new culture and people. He was not only impressed by the Kung fu but was more curious about the people, language, and the culture in that movie and he came to knew that, the movie was about Chinese culture. Through a long struggle he managed to arrange a rented black and white TV, VCR and Video Cassettes of *Snake in the Eagle Shadow* and some other Chinese culture based movies and watched over and over again and started to learn about china.

That seven-year-old boy was me and later I started reading about Chinese culture, Chinese stories, Chinese paintings and music's. Within my limited resources I have been passionately following my curiosity about Chinese culture, Language and people. Since the begging of my curiosity in 1990 and until now movies played major role to visualize my understanding about china and it was more a romanticized image of China I have created in my mind. But later years books and other readings gave clearer picture of Chinese culture and history. Because of same curiosity I have decided to study international relations to know more about culture and history mainly Chinese history. Throughout my learning life Chinese Civilization and Culture inspired me and no other culture stimulated my inquisitiveness of knowledge. I started my study about China from the Chinese Yellow River civilization and history of Silk Road.

Ever since the human started to live together and moved from one place to another for survival civilization have formed and each groups have developed their own culture of survival, settlements, cultivation, hunting, art, ideas and engineering etc,. As we know there were different civilizations across the world, such as Mesopotamia, Egyptian, Yellow river of Chinese, Greek, Indus valley and many others. But the Yellow River civilization encouraged my attention.

Records of the Grand Historian (史记) and *Bamboo Annals* (竹书纪年) gave the information about 4000 year old Chinese civilization and the vague information of Xia dynasty (2000-1600 BC) even before Shang Dynasty (1600-1050 BC) and Zhou Dynasty (1050-200 BC) who ruled the Yellow river valley. In 221 BC the Qing Dynasty consolidated many small kingdoms in the region and built up a single massive empire and become the first emperor of China under emperor Qin Shihuang. During the same time conquest of Alexander reached up to India to widen his empire for trade and wealth. But western emperors did not conquered china because of its uniqueness of the culture and the mysterious geography.

Silk Road have found out since the 12th century BC and during the Han dynasty the western explorers marked the land of china as Serica. During Han Dynasty the cross border trade culture practiced and during this period Zhang Qian-envoy to the western region was deployed by Emperor Hanwu of Han Dynasty and later this route developed as the classical silk rout in Eurasian region. The evidence has shown that there was mass production of silks during Han Dynasty period and carried away for trade. Discovery of paper revolutionized the international trade in the ancient world it enriched silk rout trade and travel. Caravan and traders used this route to trade, explore and exchange the ideas and culture between this people. From China products like Silk, tea, porcelain, paper, gun powder, and iron carried through India, Arabian Peninsula, Middle East, Africa and Europe.

Modern China

China was attacked by Japan in 1937 and slaughtered more than 14 million people and the fought lasted long 8 years, it was the longest world war slaughter field Japan. The innocent children, women and men were killed by mass bombing and it was one of the biggest massacre in the history of the world was happened in Nanking, China. It was a painful reading days in my life when I gone through forgotten holocaust did by the Japan in Nanjing. But as phoenix from the ashes, China re-emerged in to the power after the establishment of Peoples republic of china in 1949 under the leadership of Chairman Mao.

In 2013, March 14th when Xi Jinping became the president of People Republic of China, China reached its modern golden age of development and growth. One Belt One Road initiative is an innovative idea forwarded by Chinese president Xi Jinping in 2013, which is focusing on a paradigm shift in international trade and culture relations. The unique feature of this idea is to connect different culture and trade together and make multi centered world with mutual learning and mutual beneficial peaceful world. Apart from International organizations and multi- tri lateral relation between the countries, one belt one road initiative is china's future global vision and a creative plan to bridge a cross border peaceful relations between china to all over the world. Initiative is planning to connect a larger network which will connect 60 countries across this area.

Current international system had created a big gap between the countries and some countries become poorer and unimportant in global trade as well as cultural field. But President Xi Jinping visionary initiative gives equal platform for all the countries to develop and become prosperous through mutual benefit policy. Today, Even the western super power can't compete with china in terms of economy, production growth, exporting goods, construction, Job creation and employment production, prosperity and people life growth. We can say that, an individual cannot complete his day without using Chinese product anywhere in the world. From small tiny products to giant products, we cannot even imagine the diversity of technology and products that china is producing. From a small street seller in India to giant business companies in US were doing business with help of Chinese production and creativity. So today China became an integral and inevitable part of world society.

So, My China story is about my curiosity and my journey through the history, culture and civilization of China and it is always an inspiration to excavate and understand its fascinating knowledge. A journey through 2000 years of antiquity beyond legends, understanding of dynasties, tremendous and unimaginable amount of art works, flourishing civilizations that nevertheless died out and disappeared in the past. It was journey to heart of unknown and attractive geography, art, language and culture of china, the land of extraordinary paintings and handicrafts, multitude of cultural influences, diversity of religions, beliefs, thoughts and so on. In my years of informal as well as academic knowledge Chinese civilization and culture are the richest in the world and modern china is the most powerful country in the world in all terms.

我的中国之旅

［亚美尼亚］龙伊沙
中国文化与科技中心主任

我对中国的了解始于 8 岁，当时我阅读了一本关于中国瓷器与丝绸制造秘密的书，书上有着许多有趣的、五颜六色的图片。多年来，我与中国外交官共事并成了朋友。我和我的朋友们在亚美尼亚第一次组织了关于中

国的书展，第一次举办了由亚美尼亚音乐家演奏的中国中世纪音乐的音乐会，制作了第一本亚美尼亚语—俄罗斯语—英语—中文手册，分别用亚美尼亚和拼音撰写，同时，我也用中文翻译了一些流行的亚美尼亚歌曲等。

我一生中访问了许多西方国家，比如俄罗斯，但是第一次访问中国却给我留下了深刻的印象。2005 年，我到了中国的宁波和上海。记得当时我们晚上十点半到达宁波，城市的街道通明但空无一人，几乎所有的大楼都是漆黑的。

似乎太奇怪了，同行的外国人询问陪同我们的中国志愿者，“人们都去哪里了？这个城市还好吧？”志愿者解释道，城市里面的人都入睡了，因为第二天也是工作日，所以人们必须要早起。后来，我在别的城市也看到了类似的情景，也正是在那个时候，我第一次意识到中国人民的责任心和勤劳精神。

从宁波到上海的旅途中，我们目睹了荒废破败的村庄旁边修建着崭新漂亮的新房。由于所有楼房的建筑都很相似，因此在旧村落旁边修建新的村庄显得格外分明，很可能这只是一个普通的社区规划。

2012 年，我在乌鲁木齐看见了同样的画面，不过在范围上更大。我还看到了漂亮的大楼而不是黏土土屋，看到了着装朴素的维吾尔族人也在使用最新样式的手机，这表明在普通大众都在体验最新科技。我也询问过维吾尔族出租车司机，平均每月能挣多少钱，他回答说，按汇率计算，每个月大约有 600 美元（这个价钱是在乌鲁木齐买一件貂皮大衣的价钱）。于是我明白了，中国是一个真正的社会主义国家——而这正是世界上许多国家所刻意追求的。

让我们回到第一次旅行吧。2005 年，当我访问上海时，我有一种强烈的感觉，我似乎在时间机器的帮助下来到了一个未来世界。美丽的建筑矗立在城市中心，精致的景观设计，多层立交的宽阔大道，这些都令人十分惊讶。有的建筑，在第三十层楼安装有凯旋门，或者有瀑布从第二十层的水平面上滑落到玻璃上，注入一个有小鱼和花的小池塘，抑或是倾泻入一个特别的巨大立方体中。

但最重要的是，我对中国官员和普通民众十分满意，他们乐于合作，有高度组织性，既友好又好客。我从中国学到了很多，工作高效、简洁明了，具有较强的信息分析能力，实施项目执行力强等。同时，我也致力于拉近亚美尼亚和中国关系。

我真的希望我能更好地汲取中国的优秀经验，与志同道合的人一起，为亚美尼亚与中国数千年友好关系注入新的活力。

My Journey in China

Izabella Muradyan / Armenia

Chinese Center of Culture and Science, Director

My acquaintance with China took place at the age of eight, when I read a book about the secrets of porcelain and silk production in China with many interesting and colorful pictures. Already being an adult, I was a friend and worked with Chinese diplomats many years (till now). I along with my friends organized the first book exhibition in Armenia about China, a concert of medieval Chinese music performed by Armenian musicians, the creation of the first Armenian-Russian-English-Chinese phrase book with Armenian transcription and pinyin, translation of popular Armenian songs in Chinese, etc.

During my life I have visited many Western countries, Russia, but my first visit to China was the most impressive. We visited Ningbo and Shanghai in 2005. We arrived in Ningbo at 22:30, the streets of the city were brightly illuminated, but almost empty and windows of buildings were mostly dark.

It seemed strange, and foreigners asked the Chinese volunteers accompanying us-where are the people, all right in the City? They explained that the City is sleeping because the next day is also working day and people have to get up early. Later, I watched a similar picture in other cities as well, but exactly at that time I firstly realized that the Chinese people are very responsible and hardworking.

During the trip from Ningbo to Shanghai, we saw dilapidated ruined villages, and right next to them new and beautiful houses were built. As the architecture for all houses was the similar, it became clear that the new villages were simply built up next to the old villages and most likely this is a general social project.

In 2012 in Urumqi I saw the same picture, but on a much larger scale. Along with the new beautiful buildings instead of clay earth houses, it was visual that even poorly dressed Uighurs used cell phones of the latest modifications, which indicates the availability of the latest technology for the general public. I also asked the Uighur taxi driver how much he earn on average, he answered, and at the exchange rate it makes around $ 600 per month (the cost of one mink fur coat in the same place, in Urumqi). Then it became clear to me that China is really a social country as it happens in many countries of the world.

Let's come back to the first trip. When I visited Shanghai (2005), I had a strong feeling that I transferred to the future with the help of time machine. Beautiful architecture in the city center and a special landscape design, multistory overpasses of wide avenues were fascinating and caused a shock. A building with a triumphal arch at the level of the 30th floor, or a waterfall sliding on the glass from the level of the 20th floor, pouring into a small pond with little fishes and flowers or a huge cube somehow taken out of the building and many other unique architectural masterpieces...

But most of all, I was again pleased with the Chinese - both government officials and ordinary people, who are open for cooperation, highly organized, friendly and hospitable. I learned a lot from the Chinese-speed in work, clarity, ability to draw up a wide range of analytical information, implementing projects for short deadlines, etc. I did much to bring Armenia closer to China. I really hope that I will be able to better study the Chinese experience and, together with like-minded people, breathe the new energy into the many thousands years relations between Armenia and China.

中国，给予我无限快乐的国家

［白俄罗斯］苏琪
明斯克国立语言大学教师

当时我 19 岁，一个年轻的大二学生，生活才刚刚开始。那时，我的生活只是例行公事。我所做的只是学习、学习、再一次……学习。我没有时间为我的家人，为我的朋友，甚至为我自己考虑。这不是生活，而是生存。我非常的不开心，对自己的生活很不满意。无论何时，只要能短暂休息，我总会在梦里畅游。

有一天，我坐在去南京的飞机上，从梦中醒来，明白这是现实。这是我的第一次飞行，而且我必须独自经历这一切，但我并不紧张，我是在期待，改变的翅膀正在挥动。

我可以肯定地说，在中国，我是活着的，而且不仅仅是活着。我享受每一件小事。

在中国，我有很多初体验。我坐在厦门的海滩上，思考着它是多么的强大有力，但同时它又是如此的温柔平静。我看着海浪亲吻沙滩，我想永远待在那里。

你也许会笑话我，我第一次看到山也是在中国。他们是如此雄伟，如此坚不可摧。我感觉自己如此渺小，如此脆弱。当你看到这样的事情时，

你就会开始明白，你所有的问题和烦恼都是过眼云烟。山是最好的抗抑郁良药。

我在中国结交了很多不同国籍的朋友，但我最好的朋友是“宿舍的屋顶”。我几乎每天晚上都来这里看南京。我既看到冰冷、雄伟的摩天大楼，也发现小巧、舒适的房屋。每当夜幕降临时，整个城市也沉睡；太阳升起时，整个城市也醒来。温暖，柔和的风在拥抱着我，我感觉到雨和鲜花的气息。我和这个城市在默默地分享秘密，我爱上了它，我希望这种爱是相互的。

因为这次到中国的经历，我改变了很多。现在我知道快乐是什么滋味了。我希望有一天我能再次体验到这种永恒的幸福。

The Country Where I was Endlessly Happy

Vilena Tsurankova / Belarus
Minsk State Linguistic University, Teacher

I was 19 at that time, a young provincial sophomore, who has just started her way in this life. At that point, my life was a routine. All I did was studying, studying and one more time… studying. I had no time for my family, for my friends and even for myself. It wasn't life, it was a survival. I was deeply unhappy and dissatisfied with my life. But whenever I had rare minutes to rest, I was dreaming.

One day I woke up from my dream just to understand that it was a reality. It was when I got up on the plane to Nanjing. My very first flight and I had to go through this all alone, but I didn't feel nervous, I was in anticipation, the wing of changes was blowing.

I can say for sure, in China I was living, not just surviving. I was enjoying every small thing.

In China I saw sea for the first time. I was sitting on the beach in Xiamen and thinking how enormous and powerful it was, but at the same time it was so gentle and calming. I watched waves kissing sand and I wanted to stay there forever.

You would laugh, but the first time I saw mountains was also in China. They were so huge, so impregnable. I felt so tiny, so vulnerable. When you see something like this, you begin to understand that all your problems and worries are such a mess. Mountains are the best antidepressants ever.

I made a lot of friends of different nationalities in China, however, my very best friend was a rooftop of my dormitory. I came there almost every evening to watch Nanjing from above. I saw cold, mighty skyscrapers and small, cozy houses, I watched the city fall asleep as the night fell and wake up the sun was rising. Warm, soft wind was embracing me, I felt the smell of rain and flowers. Me and the city were sharing secrets silently, I fell in love with it, and I hope this love was mutual.

I've changed a lot due to this time in China. Now I know what it's like to be happy. And I hope one day I'll be able to experience this feeling of eternal bliss once again.